OFF THE HOOK

A Cook's Tour of Coastal Connecticut

PRESENTED BY

The Junior League of Stamford-Norwalk, Inc.

JLSN BOOKS

Darien, Connecticut

1989

Illustrations and Book Design by Amy Lamb

The purpose of the Junior League is exclusively educational
and charitable and is to promote voluntarism, to develop the potential
of its members for voluntary participation in community affairs,
and to demonstrate the effectiveness of trained volunteers.

The Junior League of Stamford-Norwalk, Inc. is open to all young
women, between the ages of 20-40, regardless of race, color,
religion or national origin, who demonstrate an interest in and
commitment to voluntarism.

Proceeds from the sale of OFF THE HOOK will be used to support community
projects sponsored by the Junior League of Stamford-Norwalk, Inc.

For additional copies, use the order forms at the back of the book or write directly
to:
OFF THE HOOK
JLSN Books
The Junior League of Stamford-Norwalk, Inc.
748 Post Road
Darien, Connecticut 06820

Suggested retail price $14.95 plus shipping charges of $1.75.
Connecticut residents add $1.12 sales tax.

FIRST EDITION
First Printing: 10,000 copies. May, 1988
Second Printing: 10,000 copies. May, 1989

Library of Congress Cataloging-in-Publication Data

Junior League of Stamford-Norwalk.
Off the hook.

1. Cookery (Seafood) 2. Cookery--Connecticut.
3. Connecticut--Social life and customs. I. Title.
TX747.J87 1988   641.6'92   88-773
ISBN 0-9619402-0-4

Designed by Amy Lamb
Typeset by Lettick Typografic, Inc., Bridgeport, Connecticut
Printed by
WIMMER BROTHERS
Memphis   Dallas

THE COOKBOOK COMMITTEE

Co-Chairmen

Jane T. Ahrens   Jane H. Gamber

Committee Members

Donna McL. Armstrong
Karen M. Aylward
Caroline T. Garrity
Caroleen M. Hughes
Sarah M. Hacala
Daria C. Kamford
Cindy S. Mabry

Carol C. McDermott
Lise N. O'Haire
Sharon P. Phillips
Susan E. Putze
Leslie V. Shaffer
Susan S. Tewksbury
Laurie E. Williamson

Acknowledgements

Many thanks to the hundreds of League members and their friends who donated so many of their favorite recipes and to the many dedicated recipe testers who carried on from there. We are also grateful to Newman's Own, Stew Leonard, Martha Stewart, Neil Sedaka, and to the many restaurants and fish stores who willingly submitted recipes. Our special thanks go to Brooke Dojny for her good ideas, sensible advice and editorial expertise; Melanie Barnard for her editorial expertise as well; Amy Lamb for her artistic creativity and design expertise; Ellen Rolfes of Rolfes & Associates for getting us off on the right foot; Donna Pintek; Debby Zindell; John Mc-Connell; Russell Shaffer; John Harmon of the Maritime Center at Norwalk; Dick Alley of the *Westport News*; The Norwalk Seaport Association; Len Harris of the Norwalk *Hour*; John H. Volk of the State of Connecticut's Department of Agriculture-Aquaculture Division; Robert A. Jones of the State of Connecticut's Bureau of Fisheries; *The Westerly Sun*; the National Fisheries Education and Research Foundation; Marion E. Richard and Gary W. Pierce of Lettick Typografic, Inc.; Sheryn Jones of Wimmer Brothers; and to the many bookstores and fish markets who gave us countless amounts of invaluable advice.

CONTRIBUTORS

Our sincere appreciation to the members of the Junior League of Stamford-Norwalk, Inc. and their friends and relatives who submitted over 350 seafood recipes. Similarity of content and space limitations prevented us from including all the recipes.

Betty Mudd Ainslie
Deborah B. Anderson
Eleanor Ayers
Karen M. Aylward
Thomas J. Aylward

Wendy Baker
Melanie Barnard
Mary Ann Barr
Lynn M. Benson
Catherine J. Biewen
Elizabeth Boscaino
Chef John Braun,
    Le Cog Hardi
    Restaurants,
    Ridgefield &
    Stamford
Alice Brooks
Karen Brossard
Nancy Luick Bryan
Susan Buchheit
Frances Buckley
Janet R. Burd
Carol Burket
Bromleigh K. Burton
Barbara Busskohl

Audrey C.
    Cadwallader
Chef Anthony
    Calabrese, The
    Ferns, New Milford
Elizabeth Parker
    Chapin
Alison M. Clark
Hal Clark
Karen Clark
Barbara B. Collins

Gretchen Collins
Jane Copeland
Phyllis T. Corcoran

Catherine S. Dee
    "Denny"
Elizabeth R. Dever
Sue Devine
Brooke Dojny
Judy Domkowski
Martha J. Durkin

Beth Eaton
Barbara Erickson
Cynthia Ervin

Peggy Faldi
Elizabeth Fenton
Alina Fonteneau
Ruth Frangopoulos
K. C. Fuller

Susan B. Gane
Bruna Gensdarmes of
    Le Mistral
    Restaurant,
    Stamford
Judith Gibbons
Joyce Gould
Adelaide Greco
Jackie Greiner
Gregory's Cafe,
    Fairfield
Ann T. Gustavson

Sara M. Hacala
Kathleen Halsey
Wendy Hansen

Diana Hanslip
Dyan Hattub
Dorothy Helgesson
Nancy Helmig
Sandra M.
    Henneberry
Beverly Hennessey
John Hightower of
    Wild Thyme Farm
    and Executive
    Director of
    Maritime Center
Doris M. Hock
Patricia Olvany
    Hodson
Patricia Going
    Holmberg
A. E. Hotchner

Beryl Ierardi

A. Marijke Janeway
Lori G. Jaros
Jan Jones
Chef Kelley G. Jones,
    Sterling Ocean
    House, Stamford
Chef Anthony Jucha of
    Bourbon Street
    Restaurant,
    Stamford

Daria Kamford
Nancy Kelley
Jan H. Kenna
Barbara H. Kennedy
Nora F. Kennedy
June Kiley

Audrey M.
   Knowbloch
Stew Leonard's
Lawrence Lewis
Cricket Lockhart
Chef Greg Loundes,
   J.F. O'Connell's
   Restaurant,
   Bridgeport
Becky K. Lovejoy

Barbara H. Macaulay
David Macaulay
Ginny Macaulay
Bridget A.
   MacConnell
Annette Maiberger
Susan C. Maloney
Gail Mapel
Susan N. Marshall
Maryland Seafood
   Cookbook
Bill Mathews
Diana Wallace
   McConnell
Dorothy H.
   McConnell
Marcie McGovern
Suzanne T. McGovern
Carol McLaren
Tina Meshberg of
   Water Street
   Restaurant, S.
   Norwalk
Kathleen S. Millard
Dale Morena
Mary Ann Mullen
Suzanne Mulrain
Mary Jane Murphy
Diane Musicaro

Frances E. Nitschke

Debby Oakley

Jack O'Connell, J.F.
   O'Connell's Pub,
   Bridgeport
Carol Oram
Larry Otter

Jill Park
Anne Pollex
Lyn Powers

Pinny Randall
Dorothy C. Raymond
Linda Ides Reardon
Renie Reiss
Martha Rheim
Kathy Olvany Riordan
Robert J. Riordan
Patricia M. Risher
Irene Robinson
Polly Roessler
Jayne M. Rogers
Joseph G. Rossi, M.D.
Paula A. Ryan

Jacqueline A. Salvo
Alice Sample
Patricia A. Scanlon
Jane Seagrave
Leba and Neil Sedaka
Leslie Shaffer
Wendell L. Shaffer
Midge Shepard
Sherrie Sorenson
Bruce L. Sprague,
   M.D.
Trina Stephenson
Gail Stewart
Martha Stewart

Oliver D. Tartaglia,
   Fishermen's Net,
   Darien
Susan Tewksbury
Nancy Toothaker
Emma Tracy

Bonnie N. Walker
Donna Walker
Joan Walker
Dale S. Wells
Jean Wells
Trisha White
Bonny Willett
Jean Winder
Karen N. Wood

Jo-Ann Zbytniewski

Contents

Introduction

It is with great pride that the Junior League of Stamford-Norwalk, Inc. presents OFF THE HOOK: *A Cook's Tour of Coastal Connecticut*.

The story of this cookbook is the story of a "minnow" turned "whale." For over six years our Junior League has been actively involved in funding and implementing parts of Norwalk's Maritime Center, and the genesis of the cookbook was a suggestion to prepare a simple seafood recipe pamphlet to hand out to Maritime Center visitors. Word of the search for pamphlet ideas and recipes spread and the enthusiasm generated was abundant and fervent. The minnow quickly evolved into a whale, and the concept of the cookbook was born. A committee formed, and recipes were solicited and double tested. These that we present herewith were chosen from over 350 seafood recipes submitted by League members, friends, relatives, local celebrities, area fish markets and restaurants.

Seafood industries have long been a vital part of the communities in our League's geographic area—indeed of the entire Connecticut coast. The Connecticut Bureau of Fisheries estimates that presently over 2600 metric tons of seafood are harvested annually from Connecticut coastal waters. Also, today more people than ever are eating fish because it tastes good *and* it is very good for you. Research has shown that eating large quantities of fish can have very beneficial effects in losing weight, lowering cholesterol and preventing heart disease. Our own market research showed us that consumption of fish nationwide will grow even more over the years to come. Given these reasons, it made a great deal of sense for us to produce this regional seafood cookbook, the proceeds from which will be returned to benefit directly the Connecticut coastline communities in which our League has undertaken or underwritten projects such as the Norwalk Maritime Center.

OFF THE HOOK is more than a collection of recipes. Our contributors communicate an enthusiasm for fish cookery that probably stems from their love for the ocean itself, especially that of coastal Connecticut. We wish to share some of that enthusiasm with the cooks, readers, and travelers who will buy this book.

Although Connecticut is the third smallest state in the U.S., it has nonetheless a wealth of interest, variety, and beauty. On Long Island Sound, there are over 250 miles of coastline and seashore, stretching from southwestern-most Greenwich to Stonington on the Rhode Island border. The land adjacent to the shoreline is nicely varied, with coves, harbors and rivers flowing into the Sound. Lovely beaches, rocks, and cliffs abut the shore. An appealing variety of historic villages and lovely resorts share the coast with prosperous suburban towns and large cities. From each area and from over 300 years of Connecticut coast fishing, oystering, and whaling, our seafaring lore and traditions have sprung. Bits of all this lore, too, we are pleased to acquaint you with throughout this book.

You will also find a chapter entitled, "A Fish Primer." In it we provide many of the basics about finfish and shellfish, from purchasing to presentation at your table.

Our aim has been to offer unusual recipes, not ones that are found in basic cookbooks. We have edited all recipes for completeness, clarity, and simplicity. Whether you are a beginner or an expert at fish cookery, we hope these recipes bring you as much pleasure and good eating as they have us.

May you enjoy reading and using this book as much as we have enjoyed creating it!

THE COOKBOOK COMMITTEE

★ Recipes we have found to be particularly outstanding have been starred throughout the book.

Stonington

Stonington, home port for Connecticut's largest commercial fishing fleet, is a charming village whose streets are lined with architectural gems. Greek Revival and Federal styles predominate, built by wealthy sea captains and merchants. The more modest homes in the village were built by the local fishermen.

Quaint shops and galleries border Water Street in the "borough" as it is known to locals. The town's former lighthouse, originally built in 1823, is now a museum. In Cannon Square, the actual cannons which repelled a British raid on Stonington's harbor, can be viewed. Commercial fishing vessels can be seen unloading their catch at the town dock or sailing from Stonington's deep protected harbor.

The Blessing of the Fleet is an annual two day event held in July. A lobster feast and dancing on the dock to live music begins the celebration. On Sunday, a parade winds through the village streets in the company of a statue of Saint Peter, the patron saint of fishermen. Local Portuguese, attired in authentic costumes, perform their native dances in the streets. The procession ends at the Fishermen's Memorial on the dock where the Bishop of Norwich praises those men who face the perils and risks of the sea. The community band plays the Sailor's Hymn—"Eternal Father, Strong to Save"—and the Bishop boards the gaily decorated flagship of the fleet. As each vessel in turn passes by, the Bishop bestows a blessing on the boat and its crew.

The parade of boats then heads out to Fishers Island Sound—the engines are cut and the Bishop reads a prayer in honor of fishermen who have been lost in a struggle to wrest a living from the sea. A wreath in the shape of a broken anchor is then cast onto the waters. An honor guard fires a volley and the surrounding fishing and lobster boats sound their horns in unison before they make their way back to Stonington's docks.

A FISH PRIMER

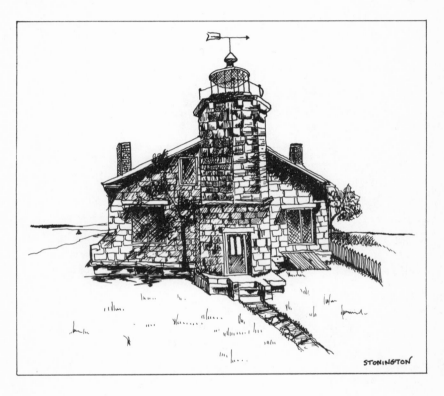

STONINGTON

FISH IS GOOD FOR YOU & YOUR HEART

Why should you include more fish in your diet? Aside from the pleasures of cooking and eating it, adding more fish to one's diet makes good nutritional sense. Most seafood is low in total fat, saturated fat and cholesterol; high in protein; low in calories; low in sodium; and is a good source of vitamins and minerals. It can also lower your risk of heart disease (still our nation's number one killer), heart attacks and strokes.

Numerous studies have linked eating seafood with a low incidence of heart disease. For instance, Eskimos living in Greenland have a very low rate of heart disease despite their heavy diet of fatty fish. The same is true of Japanese fishermen. As a result of these and other studies, medical scientists have discovered that eating a goodly amount of fish seems to have an apparent protective effect on the heart and blood vessels.

The fat that is found in seafood (particularly in the fatty fishes) is made up in large part of "omega-3 fatty acids," a type of highly polyunsaturated fat. These fatty acids can actually lower blood levels of triglycerides and cholesterol and reduce both the numbers and stickiness of blood platelets, making the blood less likely to clot. Also they aid in preventing the build-up of arterial cholesterol deposits which restrict the flow of blood through the arteries. Numbers of cardiologists now recommend that fatty fish and shellfish take the place of meat, poultry and cheese three or more times a week. The fatty fish are those with high levels of omega-3 acids and they include: tuna, mackerel, salmon, bluefish, sardines, rainbow trout, herring, shad and pompano. It is also interesting to note that shellfish which are very low in fat, nonetheless do contain large amounts of these fatty acids. Shellfish are not the high cholesterol producing foods they were once thought to be. Also, the low fat content of shellfish makes it desirable food for people concerned about their weight as well as their hearts. If you decide to add more fish to your diet, here are a few pointers on nutrition.

1. Seafood is an excellent source of complete protein. In fact, a single serving of fish can provide a large portion of your daily protein needs.

2. A number of fish are good sources of essential minerals and trace elements. Sardines, canned salmon, and mackerel are rich in calcium. Clams and oysters are rich in iron. Also seafood in general is a good source of B vitamins.

3. Fresh fish is generally very low in sodium. However, many canned varieties are extremely salty. Look for brands that have either low sodium or no salt.

4. Buy only canned fish that is packed in water or tomato sauce. Those packed in oil are much higher in calories and in saturated fat content.

5. Be careful of smoked fish. While many of the fatty fishes can be purchased smoked, the smoking process makes them very high in salt which can in turn raise blood pressure.

6. Fish dishes that are breaded and fried often contain more bread than fish as well as lots more fat. Remember also that the greatest loss of nutrients occurs when fish is fried.

7. The best ways to prepare fish if you are watching cholesterol and caloric intake are: baking, broiling (retains nearly all the natural nutrients), poaching and steaming. Avoid fish that is prepared with rich and fatty sauces.

JUDGING FRESHNESS

Smell, looks, and feel will tell you quickly whether the fish you're about to buy is really fresh. And with fish cookery, freshness is key to insuring good texture and fine flavor.

Whether fish is whole or cut, it must smell clean and fresh, with *no* "fish" or other unsavory odor! If whole, the fish must have bright, clear, protruding eyes, pink gills (not dull grey-brown), and scales or skin that is taut and shining. Fish steaks or fillets should appear bright, clean, and even-textured, without any trace of yellow or brown at their edges. To the touch, whole or cut fish should feel firm and moist—if it's slippery or slimy or the skin doesn't stick to the fish, don't buy it.

Frozen fish should show no discoloration, no frost or freezer burn, and ideally will appear in a tightly wrapped package that is frozen solid without air space. When properly frozen fresh fish has defrosted, it should compete favorably with the fresh fish described above. Any strong odor, shredding, or yielding of liquid when pressed means poor quality.

Shellfish (lobster, shrimp, oyster, clam, mussel, etc.), especially if sold without the shell, should smell clean and fresh and should look the natural color of their cooked or uncooked state. (Do ask if in doubt.) Since storage of certain shellfish is generally difficult, it is best to buy lobsters, crabs, oysters, clams and mussels that are alive for best cooking results. And do not hesitate to reject oysters, clams, mussels, and other bi-valves if the shell is open or moves easily; soft-shell clams are an exception—their shells always gap a bit.

MARKET FORMS AND BUYING GUIDE

Term	Meaning	Approx. amt. required per person

For Fish:

Term	Meaning	Approx. amt. required per person
Whole, or round	Sold just as it comes from the water. Check the recipe to see if a "whole" fish might mean a whole "dressed" fish (see below).	1 lb.
Drawn, or cleaned	Whole fish that has been gutted and possibly has had scales and gills removed.	¾ lb.
Dressed	Whole fish with entrails, scales, gills, fins, head and tail removed. Usually the backbone remains.	½ lb.
Pan-dressed	A small dressed fish (with or without its tail) that may have had its backbone removed. Ready for sauteeing or deep-frying.	½ lb.
Steak	Dressed fish (backbone remains) that is cross-cut into 1″ slices for broiling, baking, steaming or poaching.	½ lb.
Fillet (also "filet")	A side of fish cut lengthwise from head to tail without any bone (with or without skin). A "butterfly" fillet is a double fillet joined along the backbone; a "kited" fillet is the same but joined along the belly.	½ lb.
Finger	A narrow piece of steak or fillet, usually frozen, used for deep-frying.	½ lb.

For Shellfish:

Term	Meaning	Approx. amt. required per person
Shucked	Uncooked shellfish (usually oysters or clams) sold without their shells.	¼-½ pint
Peeled, deveined shrimp	Raw, headless shrimp with shell and black vein removed. Can be fresh or frozen.	Number depends on the size of the shrimp.
Live	The best way to buy lobster and crab so they can be cooked fresh. Also sold cooked, in or out of the shell.	½-1 lb. meat per person
On the shell	Clams, oysters, mussels eaten raw from their shells.	1-2 doz.

Fish & Shellfish Varieties

The following is a compendium of common fin fish and shellfish varieties available in fish markets along the Connecticut coast. Included under each fish species is information such as its popular names, its market forms, and some interesting facts.

Angler

- Monkfish, Sea Devil
- Boneless tail, fillets
- Only the thick tail sections of this fish are edible. It has a mild, sweet flavor not unlike lobster.

Bluefish

- Whole, dressed, fillets
- Bluefish does not freeze well. Fillets have a dark strip down the center which has a strong fishy flavor. To remove, cut a shallow V along each side of the strip and lift it out, being careful not to cut through the fillet.
- Available late spring through fall.

Catfish

- Whole, dressed, fillets, smoked
- Most catfish are aquacultured in Mississippi, though some are caught in the Great Lakes, other lakes and inland rivers. Catfish have tough skins that must be removed.

Clams

- Littleneck
  Soft Shell (a.k.a. steamers)
  Quahog (a.k.a. chowder clams)
- Live in shell, shucked (fresh or frozen), canned

Crabs

- Blue (Soft-shell)
  Alaskan King
  Stone
- Live in shell (for soft-shell), fresh or frozen, lump meat or whole claws
- Blue crab is the major catch along the Atlantic and Gulf coasts; King crab comes from the frigid waters off the Pacific Northwest coast; Stone crab from the waters off Florida.

Crawfish

- Live or cooked in the shell
- These small freshwater crustaceans are found in rivers and estuaries, mostly in Louisiana. Most of the meat is found in the tail.

Drum/Croaker

- Redfish
- Whole, dressed, fillets
- Redfish has been made popular by Louisiana chefs.

Eel

- Whole, smoked
- Eel is a snake-like fish with a tough skin that must be removed before cooking.

Flounder/Sole

- Dover Sole
  English Sole (Lemon Sole)
  Fluke (Summer Flounder)
  Gray Sole
  Winter Flounder
- Whole, dressed, fillets
- Flounder and sole are the best-known fish in the U.S. All of the soles, with the exception of the European Dover sole, are actually varieties of flounder.

Haddock

- Whole, dressed, fillets, steaks, smoked
- Haddock is closely related to cod, though it is usually smaller. It can be used interchangeably in recipes.

Halibut

- Whole, fillets, steaks
- This is the largest of the flatfish/flounders, and is usually more expensive.

Herring

- Whole, pickled, salted, smoked
- Fresh herring is rarely available. The smoked varieties are known as sardines.

Lobsters

- Live or cooked in the shell, whole or tails, canned
- Lobsters are found in virtually all continental shelf areas. As late as the 1800's, lobster was so common it was used for fish bait. Times have changed!

Mackerel

- Atlantic Blue, Spanish, King
- Whole, dressed, fillets, steaks, smoked
- Available late spring through fall.

Mahi Mahi

- Dolphin fish
- Steaks, fillets
- Do not think this is the mammal dolphin! This large, edible fish is found in tropical and sub-tropical waters.

Mussels

- Live in shell, canned, smoked
- The Atlantic mussels are the most common variety and they are found in abundance off the coast. Increasing numbers, however, are being farmed. They are raised on ropes, which keep them off the sea bottom and hence, they are clean and sand-free.

Ocean Perch

- Redfish, Red Perch, Rosefish
- Whole, fillets
- Fillets are usually sold with the skin on.

Oysters

- Live in shell, shucked, canned, smoked
- About 90 million pounds of these mollusks are eaten each year! Eastern or Atlantic oysters are taken from the waters off the Atlantic coast. Their names usually indicate the area from which they came, such as Blue Point, Cape Cod, Long Island, Chincoteague, Cotuit and Apalachicola.

Pollock

- Atlantic Pollock, Blue Cod, Boston Bluefish
- Whole, dressed, fillets, steaks
- Pollock is similar to cod only smaller. It can be used interchangeably in recipes.

Pompano

- Whole, dressed, fillets
- This is a very expensive and very desirable fish.

Salmon

- Sockeye, Chinook, Silver, Pink, Chum, Atlantic
- Whole, dressed, fillets, steaks, smoked, canned
- All varieties, except Atlantic, are found in the Pacific, mostly in Alaskan waters.

Scallops

- Bay, Calico, Sea, Icelandic
- Fresh or frozen, shucked
- Bay scallops are available October through March.

Scrod

- Whole, dressed, fillet
- According to the Massachusetts Division of Marine Fisheries, scrod is the market term for any fish in the cod family weighing under 2½ pounds whole.

Sea Bass

- Black Sea Bass, Striped Sea Bass
- Whole, fillets, steaks
- Striped bass is available late spring through fall. Grouper is sometimes sold as sea bass and can be used interchangeably.

Shad

- Whole, dressed, fillets, boned, smoked, canned
  Shad Roe: fresh or frozen, canned
- Shad is a very bony fish, and is valued for its roe. It is available spring through early summer.

Shark

- Mako
- Chunks, steaks
- Shark is available spring through fall and is gaining in popularity, as it tastes like swordfish but is less expensive.

Shrimp

- Nine different varieties, all tasting virtually the same!
- Fresh or frozen: raw (headless, in shell); peeled (deveined, raw or cooked); canned
- The tiny, delicious Northern Shrimp are available late-fall to mid-spring.

Smelt

- White Bait
- Whole, dressed
- Small smelt are eaten whole. Larger smelt should be headed and gutted.

Snapper

- Red Snapper, Yellowtail, Golden Snapper
- Whole, dressed, fillets
- Red snapper has a beautiful rose-colored skin and red eyes. There are other colorful snappers from the Pacific under the Rockfish species. These are often sold as "snapper" but they are not a counterpart to the real Atlantic red snapper.

Squid

- Whole, cleaned, fillets, strips, pieces
- The *Loligo* squid (winter or long fin) is available spring and early summer. The *Illex* squid (summer or short fin) is available summer to early winter.

Swordfish

- Steaks, chunks
- Available spring through fall.

Tautog

- Blackfish
- Whole, dressed, fillets
- Available spring through fall.

Tilefish

- Tile Bass
- Whole, dressed, fillets, steaks
- This somewhat unknown fish can be cooked like snapper and rockfish and is available spring through fall.

Trout

- Rainbow trout
- Dressed, smoked, boned, butterflied
- Available all year. Trout and rainbow trout are virtually the same.

Whelk

- Conch, Periwinkles
- Sold live in markets and also cooked.

Tuna

- Bluefin, Yellowfin, Skipjack, Albacore, Bonito
- Dressed, fillets, steaks, canned
- Fresh tuna is available late spring through fall.

Whitefish

- Whole, dressed, fillets, steaks, smoked
- Many people regard this as one of the best tasting freshwater fish.

CARING FOR YOUR CATCH

Make sure to carry a cooler with you on your next fishing trip. Layer the cooler with crushed ice on the bottom. When you catch a fish, simply drop the fish into the cooler and continue fishing. Gut, gill and bleed the fish as soon as possible to maintain freshness. This may be done before the fish is placed in the cooler; however, you may wait until you reach shore to clean the fish.

HOW TO CLEAN A FRESH FISH

- Hold the fish head firmly and remove its scales by scraping from the tail to the head with a scraper or the blunt edge of a knife. This may be done either before or after cleaning the fish.
- Cut out the gills with a sharp knife or kitchen shears. Gut and clean the fish from vent to head. Be sure to clean out its intestines and rinse the fish out in the lake, or stream or salt water to retard spoilage. If at home, rinse the fish with a solution of one part vinegar to three parts water.

- Remove head, gills and side fins by cutting above the collarbone and through the backbone. Trim off the flesh by holding the tail and then cut off the tail. Cut the flesh along each side of the fins to remove the dorsal and back fin. With pliers, tug towards the head of the fish and its fins with root bones will come loose.
- Wash the fish in cold, salted water.
- If the fish is not on ice, keep it in a shady area wrapped in a damp cloth or a damp newspaper.

STORING FRESH FISH

Whole fish or fillets should be tightly double-wrapped in a cling wrap, then wrapped in aluminum foil to insure that no air can reach the flesh. Thawed frozen fish or fresh fish should be stored in a cold refrigerator and cooked within one or two days.

FREEZING FISH

Freshly caught fish should be frozen immediately. Wrap fish tightly in moisture-proof freezer wrap or heavy-duty aluminum foil while wet, which allows fish to keep longer. Squeeze any air out of the package and close securely. Fish can be frozen for 4-6 months.

Fatty fish can be dipped in an ascorbic acid-and-water bath for one minute before freezing. You can mix a few soluble Vitamin C capsules in water to create this bath.

In freezing lean fish, place fish in milk cartons filled with water. Staple the top and place in the freezer. This method of freezing increases storage and does not dry out fish. Using this method, fish can be frozen as long as eight months.

Another method of preserving whole fish is known as glazing. It is done by freezing the unwrapped fish first, dipping it in water chilled with ice cubes, then re-freezing it. By repeating this process several times, the thick glaze preserves the fish indefinitely, as long as the fish is not allowed to thaw. Wrap the fish tightly to store.

When defrosting frozen fish, place your fish package in a dish and allow it to thaw in a cold refrigerator for 24 hours. Fish may also be defrosted by placing the package under cold running tapwater; however, this method causes the fish to lose some flavor.

FILLETING FISH

Fish under 10 lbs.

Lay the clean, scaled, gutted fish on a cutting board. Cut down through the meat along the back from its tail to behind the head. Then cut down the backbone to just above the collarbone. Using the ribs as a guide, cut along the backbone to the tail. Turn the fish on the other side, and repeat the steps above. Make sure that *all* the bones have been removed before cooking.

Fish over 10 lbs.

Cut behind the fish's gills and side stub to the backbone. Cut the skin near the fins and around the edge of the fillet. (An easy method is to use the knife facing out, and slide the tip along under the skin.) Starting at the gill, lift a bit of the skin and cut away where it clings to the flesh. Fillet the fish by using its ribs as a guide for the knife. Repeat the process on the other side.

Flatfish

Begin on the dark side of the fish. Cut behind the gills from the top of the head to the center backbone. Then cut down the backbone from head to tail. Turn the knife flat. Cut toward one edge, the length of the fish, using the spine as a guide. Do the same process on the other half of the dark side (which is the top part of the fish). Repeat the process on the other side of the fish (white side).

SHELLFISH

Freshness Characteristics

Common characteristics which indicate the freshness of shellfish are:

- Sea breeze odor
- Tightly closed shells for clams, mussels and oysters. If shells are slightly open, tap lightly with a knife, as they should close. Discard any shellfish that do not close.
- Tightly curled tails for lobsters (when picked up) and leg movement for live crabs and lobsters. If refrigerated, they will not be very active,

but they should move a bit.
- Mild odor for freshly shucked oysters and scallops. Smaller bay and calico scallops are usually creamy white, though they may be light tan and pink. Larger sea scallops are also creamy white, but may show pink or light orange coloration.
- Clear, slightly milky or light grey liquid around freshly shucked oysters. The oysters themselves should be creamy white in color.
- Mild odor and firm meat for shrimp.

Storing Shellfish

The storage life depends on whether the shellfish is live, frozen, thawed or freshly cooked. Shellfish should be kept as close to 32°F as possible when stored in the refrigerator. Store shrimp and shucked shellfish in a leakproof bag or covered jar. Squid and freshly shucked clams can be stored for 1 to 2 days; shrimp and scallops 2 to 3 days; and freshly shucked oysters 5 to 7 days. Mussels and clams in the shell will last 2 to 3 days. Oysters should be used within 7 to 10 days. Tap any shells open during storage. Discard those which do not close. Store live shellfish in a shallow dish covered with damp towels or even paper towels. Do not put live shellfish in an airtight container or water, as they will suffocate and die. Live lobsters and crabs should be cooked the day they are purchased. Refrigerated cooked shellfish should be used within 2 to 3 days.

Preparing Shellfish

Clams   Scrub the shells and soak several times in salt water for an hour. This encourages the clams to spit out sand and grit. Put the clams on a cookie sheet and chill in the freezer for an hour, or refrigerate. Cold clams are easier to open than warm.

Open the clams over a bowl and collect their juice. Using a thin, broad knife, and holding a clam with the hinge against the palm of your hand, insert the knife in-between the shell. Use your fingers to "pull" the knife between the shells as you close your fist. Cut around the rim to sever the abductor muscle, which is down close to

the hinge. Remove the upper shell and run the knife
under the clam to loosen it from the bottom shell. Pull its
black siphon tip and filmy siphon sheath off.

Crab

To kill a live crab, drop it into boiling water for two minutes, then run it under cold water. Holding the legs, pull
off the top shell. Turn the crab over and pull off a triangu-
lar piece of shell to remove the breastplate. Pull off its
gray feathery gills along the sides. Remove the white
intestine and grayish matter along the back. Remove the
mouth parts. (The tomalley and any roe may be used for
the flavoring of butter sauces.) Break the crab in half ver-
tically. Twist and pull off the legs and claws from the
body section.

Lobster

To kill a live lobster for grilling, insert a sharp knife crosswise where the head meets the shell to sever the spinal
cord. Turn the lobster onto its back; make a deep cut
down the body without cutting through the shell; and
open it out. Remove the black vein and stomach (near the
head). Remove and save the tomalley and roe or coral for
compound butters.

When boiling a lobster, place it head first into boiling
salted water (2 teaspoons of salt to 3 quarts of water).
Cover the pot and boil the lobster 10-12 minutes for the
first pound and one minute for each additional ¼ pound.
The shell will appear bright red when the lobster is done.

Mussels

Scrub the mussel shells. Pull out the grassy fibers hang-
ing out of the shell (the beard) with a firm tug. Soak the
mussels in cold water to loosen the sand and remove
some of the salty flavor. To open, cut the muscle holding
the shells together and separate the shells. Pull the meat
away from the beard and the tough muscle attached to it.
For large ocean mussels, take out the soft, dark center
part.

Oysters   Scrub the shells under running water. Store loosely
            wrapped in a paper bag or in a bowl in the refrigerator
            until needed. Oysters are shucked just like clams. Be
            sure the oyster liquor is clear; if it appears cloudy or
            milky, discard the oyster and its liquor.

Shrimp   To shell a shrimp, begin on the underside at the head
            end. Separate the shell and gently pull it away working
            down the tail. The shell should pull off easily. Remove
            the dark vein running down the back just under the sur-
            face with a paring knife.

Squid   Buy squid cleaned or whole. To clean, cut off the tenta-
            cles just below the eye, leaving the eye on the body.
            Wash and rub off as much of the skin as will come off.
            Squeeze out the conical beak from the opening of the
            tentacles. Press down at the head to pull it off the body
            and discard. Rinse the inky substance out of the body and
            pull out the hard quill located just inside. Pull off the pur-
            plish, transparent membrane covering the body, leaving
            the white meat to use. Drain the squid and dry on
            towels.

EQUIPMENT FOR COOKING FISH

Heat:
An oven thermometer; a fat thermometer for deep-frying.

Handling in general:
Sharp knives and small pliers for cutting and boning; kitchen shears (fish shears are also available); fish scaler; fillet knife; knife sharpener; cheesecloth for poaching, steaming, or straining broth; tongs, wide spatulas, long handled fork for testing doneness; strainer; twine and small skewers for lacing the fish after stuffing; timer for accurately timing.

For sauces, liquids, oils, etc:
Wire whisk, ladle, (wooden) spoons; fine mesh strainers; cheesecloth; pastry brush; baster.

Cooking utensils:
Wire rack with handle(s) for grilling;
Fish poacher (24" or more length) or deep pan and wire rack for poaching;
Steamer or deep pan and wire rack for steaming;
Oval oven-proof, microwave-proof casserole dishes for baking, broiling, microwaving, *and* serving at table;
Sautéeing pan for pan-frying and sauteeing;
Shallow pans for broiling;
Broiler pan for broiling;
(Iron) skillets for frying and baking;
Stockpot for stocks, soups, stews, chowders.

Handling shellfish:
Wooden mallet, sharp knife, lobster pick, nutcracker or "claw cracker" for cracking and picking crab or lobster shells;
Clam and oyster knives for shucking (a device called a "clam opener" is available);
A "shrimper" for quickly deveining and shelling all but the smallest size shrimp prior to cooking.

COOKING METHODS FOR FIN FISH

Successfully cooking fish simply means taking care to cook it enough, of course, and taking special care never to cook it too much. Refinements and subtleties in fish cookery occur with your choice of oil, juice, marinade, wine, or other liquids that both flavor the fish and prevent it from sticking to the cooking utensil; your choice of herbs or sauces that "marry well" with the fish you have chosen; and, especially for fish, your choice of one of the cooking methods that follow below.

As in the preparation of fish for any recipe in this cookbook, fish used in any of the below cooking methods should be rinsed in cool water, cleaned off, and patted dry with a paper towel.

THE CANADIAN COOKING THEORY

Most of the creatures we think of as fish are cold blooded animals. Thus, the longer they are cooked, quite opposite to their warm-blooded meat-bearing relatives, the tougher they can become. Fortunately there is a simple and nearly foolproof method for accurately cooking fish so that the fish just flakes, is still moist, but has had its raw translucent texture changed by heat to a solid white or opaque appearance at its center. Developed by the Canadian Fisheries and Marine Service, it is referred to as "the Canadian cooking theory" or, here, "the Canadian rule." The rule is easily remembered and it makes fish cookery appealingly simple and *quick*! It works like this:

1. Lay down the fish (or any cut) horizontally and measure it (depth-wise) at its thickest point. Include fractions. Measure a stuffed fish after stuffing. Measure the diameter of a rolled fillet.
2. For any of the basic methods of cooking fish explained below (except stir-frying and microwaving) the cooking time to allow is 10 minutes per inch of thickness. Count fractions here, too!
3. Rule modifications: Allow 20 minutes per inch for frozen fish. Add 5 minutes per inch if sauce is part of the cooking. Add 5 minutes per inch if the fish is cooked in paper or foil. These modifications may result in less accuracy of cooking, so check the fish carefully as it cooks.

4. The Canadian rule requires baking in a very hot oven (400° to 450°) and broiling 3″ to 4″ under a heated broiler. It is important that you check the accuracy of your oven temperature with an oven thermometer as some ovens can vary by as much as 50° from their setting.

5. The Canadian rule does not apply to: very thin cuts; soups, stews, chowders; cooking shellfish; microwave cooking or stir-frying.

CHOICE OF COOKING METHOD

You can choose a method of cooking that will set off the fish to its best, for both flavor and texture. For example, lean or white-meated fish (like trout, sole, cod, bass) are, to some tastes, better when broiled, baked, or fried. Oilier fish, such as salmon or swordfish, are excellent when baked or broiled, of course, but are thought to absorb—better than lean fish—flavors or herbs used in poaching and steaming. Also with oilier fish it is wise nutritionally to avoid cooking with any method that requires more oil, such as sautéeing or deep-frying.

Another frame of reference for choosing a cooking method is that the methods fall into some general categories, as follows:

"Dry Cooking": includes baking, broiling, grilling, oven-frying. The caution here is to see that fish does not dry out.

"Wet Cooking": includes poaching, steaming, braising. Be careful not to leave the fish in the liquid after it is cooked or it will toughen.

Frying: includes pan-frying, sautéeing, and stir-frying. These methods are not recommended for solidly frozen fish.

Deep-frying: This method actually means boiling in oil (or in any oil substitute such as butter). This method is not recommended for solidly frozen fish.

Microwave: Remember that fish is delicate. Once heated, it very nearly cooks itself, and thus more than other foods it will continue cooking after removal from the microwave oven.

If you have questions about a fish cookery method, try asking at the market where the fish was sold, consult friends or cookbooks at a library, or acknowledge cheerfully that even the best of cooks are not infallible. Although the Canadian rule is designed to relieve you from forking the fish for doneness every few minutes, you will still want to check cooking progress by sight, at least, and by testing a little before the fish is supposed to be done so as to avoid overcooking.

GENERAL EXPLANATIONS OF EACH COOKING METHOD

Baking

Preheat oven to 400 + °. Place fish (skin side down if a fillet) in well greased shallow pan. Season with herbs, salt, pepper, or lemon juice (among others) to taste, and dot or baste with butter, margarine, or oil. Cook according to the Canadian rule. Baked fish is wonderful served with a sauce or herbed butter. (Refer to Sauces chapter.)

Broiling

Preheat broiler and be certain to oil the surface on which the fish is cooked. Season and baste the fish with melted butter or margarine. Place fish 3″ to 4″ from heat (no need to turn if fish is thin); place fish 5″ or more from heat if fish is dressed or frozen (turn at least once and check often if fish has been frozen). Time the cooking by the Canadian rule and baste often with butter or oil. It's best to use fish no more than 2″ thick; otherwise the fat used in cooking will start to smoke and can eventually catch fire. Unless your oven directions state otherwise, leave the oven door slightly open. Seasoning may be added after (instead of before) cooking. Parsley sprigs and lemon slices are colorful garnishments.

Grilling

Preheat coals or wood until well started. Place fish in well oiled wire rack. Fish can also be placed on well-greased foil, or wrapped in well-greased foil approximately 6″ above coals. Time cooking by the Canadian rule and baste often. Seasoning may be added after (instead of before) cooking. Some say there is no taste in the world quite like fresh fish from the grill!

Oven-frying

This means baking at a very high temperature. Preheat oven to 500°. Bread fish with dry bread crumbs and place it in a lightly greased shallow pan. Baste with 2 tablespoons of butter (or other oil) per pound of fish. Place fish on top rack of oven; the thicker it is, the nearer the top it should be placed. Time by the Canadian rule, but check the top of the fish. If it cooks too quickly, reduce the heat, or lower the fish, or both. This is a great method for weight-watchers; the fish tastes fried, but very little oil is required compared with frying.

Poaching

If you want to be sure your fish is removable in one piece, wrap the fish in cheesecloth (wrap so as to be able to open on top to check doneness). In a fish poacher, or in a pan deep enough to have the poaching liquid cover the fish, bring poaching liquid to a boil. Standard poaching liquids include water with herbs, half water half milk, water with wine, and court bouillon. Lower the dressed or cut fish into the liquid and do not permit boiling to resume. Gently simmer for the time indicated by the Canadian rule or by your recipe. Remove carefully and serve hot or cold. Poached fish served with any mayonnaise based sauce (refer to Watercress Sauce on page 103) is really a taste treat, but this is only one way poached fish tastes fine!

A Simple Court Bouillon

2 quarts water	$1/2$ teaspoon thyme
1 cup dry white wine	2 stalks celery with leaves, sliced
1 tablespoon salt	into 2 or 3 pieces
3-4 sprigs parsley	1 carrot, coarsely chopped
1 bay leaf	4 peppercorns

Bring all of the above ingredients to a boil over high heat in a 6-quart stainless steel or enamel pot. Partially cover the pot, reduce heat and simmer for 30 minutes. Strain through a large, fine sieve and cool. NOTE: for a more highly flavored broth ideal for poaching fish to be served cold, you should add another cup of wine, $1/4$ cup of wine vinegar and 3 sliced onions to the above mixture.

Steaming

In a pan with a tight-fitting lid, place a rack above boiling water. You may wish to tie the fish in cheesecloth as for poaching (see above). Place fish on rack and cover with lid. Time by the Canadian rule.

Braising

This method involves partial poaching of fish over a bed of vegetables. Used frequently in Europe, this method yields mouth-watering results. Vegetables, such as a combination of carrots, onions, and mushrooms, are cleaned and cut into julienne strips, then softened by sautéeing in small amounts of butter or oil. The fish is arranged over the vegetables, topped with some bacon, butter, or other fat, and covered halfway up its sides with a cooking liquid (usually wine combined with water or stock). Bring the liquid to a boil quickly, then lower the heat so the fish simmers gently by the Canadian rule of timing. The fish may also be simmered (again according to the Canadian rule) in a moderate (350°) oven. Baste often with cooking liquid and use any excess liquid as an ingredient in an acompanying sauce. (Refer to Provençale Sauce for Fish on page 104.)

Pan Frying

Using seasoned crumbs, flour, or cornmeal, bread small, whole fish, fish fillets, or bite-sized chunks. Various batters also work well. Fry in hot butter, oil, or a combination of approximately one part butter to two or three parts oil, until brown on both sides. Drain on absorbent paper and serve with lemon or lime slices. Note that nutritionally speaking the recommended oils are vegetable oils high in polyunsaturated fat: corn, soybean, sunflower, and cottonseed, for example.

Sautéeing

Pan fry the fish (see above). After removing the fish to a warm platter, various combinations of seasonings, wine, stock, and butter are added to the pan to make an accompanying sauce, which is then served over the fish. (Refer to Sauce Beurre Blanc on page 105.)

Stir-frying

Together with broiling, this is one of the fastest means of cooking fish. It requires heating oil so that it is very hot in a wok or large skillet, then adding fish that has been cut into uniformly small pieces, and gently stirring until the pieces turn opaque. Combinations of seasonings, soy sauce, and vegetables are usually also cooked together with or to accompany the fish.

Deep Frying

Preheat oil in a deep pot (to avoid splattering) to 375°. Dip the fish in a batter, or in a sequence of flour, beaten egg, and bread crumbs. Place in a frying basket or drop into hot fat until browned. The cooking time will be approximately 10 minutes per inch so long as the temperature is maintained at 375°. Drain well and serve with the traditional seafood sauce of catsup and horseradish, or with tartar sauce. (See recipe for Fish Fondue on page 122.)

Microwave Cookery

Place fish on a very flat or shallow dish. Seal in juices by covering with plastic wrap (punch holes so as to vent steam) or by coating well with crumbs. Cook fillets on high power 3 to 4 minutes per pound if boneless (more if not); turn the dish halfway through cooking. Check microwave oven directions for cooking thick steaks and whole fish; usually they will require lower heat settings or other careful treatment. Remove the fish when edges are done. Allow the fish to stand to complete the cooking.

Best of luck...and best of eating!

Mystic

There was a time when ships for trade, war, whaling, fishing
and even romantic clipper ships were expertly crafted in the yards of
Mystic. Just as there was a time when sea captains lived on every street
in town, and there was no port of entry in the world where a Mystic
man had not been. Every family had souvenirs of travel and at least
one relative who had voyaged the world over. All of the talk was about
ships that were built and the men who sailed them. They spread the
legend of one Mystic captain who had made more passages around
Cape Horn than any other—at least eighty. They told stories about the
clipper *Andrew Jackson* that recorded the fastest passage of any sailing
vessel between New York and San Francisco—a mere eighty-nine days
and four hours! The life of the town was the life of the sea, and all told,
until 1900, the people of Mystic turned out some of the fastest, best
designed sailing vessels and steamships afloat.

We might not have known that Mystic was once a busy
seaport had a group of its citizens not banded together in 1929 to
preserve old maritime records and ships. From their efforts came
Mystic Seaport, one of the outstanding maritime museums in the
world.

Mystic Seaport today consists of forty or so buildings, some
of which have been moved from their original locations, to stand in
this re-created 19th century village. Nestled near wharves on cob-
bled streets are all of the services needed to outfit a ship and provide
for the needs of a town. In addition to inspecting a sail loft and rope
walk, the visitor can also stop by the church, school, tavern, and
countinghouse. A superb maritime library houses collections for the
scholar as well as the less serious student.

What makes Mystic Seaport unique is its shipyards which
restore and maintain the more than 300 vessels that it owns. Twenty
or thirty of these are on view at any one time, including the *Charles
W. Morgan*, one of the last great wooden whale ships, the *Joseph*

HORS D'OEUVRES

Conrad, and the *L.A. Dunton*. Besides galleries which exhibit scrimshaw, paintings, and other nautical memorabilia there are demonstrations of the practical arts. Festivals and special events which the Seaport stages throughout the year complement this spectacular attraction which promises a rewarding experience to each and every visitor.

★Hot Clam Dip

This is a nice hors d'oeuvre for a winter cocktail party.

2   *8-ounce packages cream cheese, softened*
2   *6-ounce cans minced clams*
⅓   *cup of clam juice (from can)*
¼   *cup minced onion*
⅛   *teaspoon cayenne*
⅛   *teaspoon black pepper*
1   *tablespoon Worcestershire sauce*
2   *tablespoons lemon juice*

1. Preheat oven to 250 degrees.
2. Combine all ingredients, mixing well to blend. (This can be done
    in the food processor.) Transfer to a baking dish or to an oven-
    to-table serving container and place in the preheated oven for 1
    hour. Serve with dip size corn chips.

PREPARATION TIME: 15 minutes
COOKING TIME: 1 hour
YIELD: 10 servings

Clam Pie

2   *6-ounce cans minced clams, including juice*
1-1½ *cups fresh bread crumbs*
¼   *pound butter, melted*
½   *teaspoon dried oregano*
½   *cup grated Parmesan cheese*
1   *small ball (8 ounces) mozzarella, grated*
        melba rounds or crackers

1. Preheat oven to 350 degrees. Combine clams, including their
    juice, with 1 cup bread crumbs, the melted butter and oregano.

Toss to combine, and add additional bread crumbs if mixture is too wet.

2. Spread into a pyrex pie plate and sprinkle with the two cheeses. Bake uncovered in the preheated oven for 20 minutes or until heated through and bubbly on top. Serve with a small knife or spoon for spreading on crackers.

PREPARATION TIME: 15 minutes
COOKING TIME: 20 minutes
YIELD: 6-8 servings

★Holiday Crabmeat Spread

Very festive and pretty for the holidays or anytime!

12 *ounces cream cheese, softened*
1   *small onion, minced*
2   *teaspoons Worcestershire sauce*
1   *pound crabmeat, picked over to remove shells and drained of excess water*
1   *cup cocktail sauce (see page 102)*
    generous ½ cup chopped pecans
3   *tablespoons chopped parsley*
    crackers

1. In a food processor or small bowl, blend together the cream cheese, onion, and Worcestershire sauce. Spread on the bottom of a 9 or 10-inch pie plate or similar serving platter.
2. Flake the crabmeat and distribute evenly over the cream cheese. Spoon cocktail sauce over crabmeat and then sprinkle with the pecans and parsley.
3. Chill until ready to serve, at least 2 hours. Serve with crackers.

PREPARATION TIME: 20 minutes (excluding chilling time)
YIELD: 12 servings

Caviar Pie

5   large hard-boiled eggs
¾   cup mayonnaise
8   ounces cream cheese, softened
½   cup sour cream
2   tablespoons lemon juice
½   cup chopped onion
1   small jar black caviar
    waffle type potato chips or small crackers for spreading

1. Butter a 9-inch pie pan.
2. Chop eggs and mix with the mayonnaise. Spread in the bottom on the buttered pan.
3. Beat cream cheese, sour cream and lemon juice until smooth. Layer on top of the egg mixture.
4. Press the onion on top of the cheese mixture and then spread the caviar over the top.
5. Refrigerate until ready to serve, at least one hour.
6. Serve with the potato chips or crackers.

PREPARATION TIME: 30 minutes (excluding chilling time)
YIELD: 12-14 servings

Lord's Point Crab Dip

1   cup mayonnaise
8   ounces crabmeat
1   teaspoon lemon juice
1   teaspoon fresh parsley
1   teaspoon sherry
    raw vegetables for dipping

1. Combine all ingredients except raw vegetables. Chill 6 hours.
2. Serve with vegetables.

PREPARATION TIME: 10 minutes (excluding chilling time)
YIELD: 2 cups

Crabmeat and Water Chestnuts

1   *pound (2 cups) crabmeat*
½   *cup chopped water chestnuts*
2   *teaspoons soy souce*
½   *cup mayonnaise*
2   *tablespoons minced green onions including green tops*

1.   Combine all ingredients and cover and refrigerate for at least an hour to blend flavors. Serve with flavorful crackers such as Rye Krisps.

PREPARATION TIME: 10 minutes
YIELD: 8 servings

Crab Deviled Eggs

8   *hard-boiled eggs, halved lengthwise*
½   *cup Hellmann's Real Mayonnaise*
1   *tablespoon Dijon mustard*
1   *tablespoon minced onion*
¾   *teaspoon dried dillweed, crushed*
½   *teaspoon grated lemon rind*
⅛   *teaspoon freshly ground pepper*
6   *ounces crabmeat*
      pimiento for garnish, optional

1.   Separate egg yolks and whites. Sieve the yolks into a mixing bowl. Reserve whites.
2.   Add remaining ingredients except pimiento to yolks and stir well. Chill at least 2 hours.
3.   Fill egg whites with crab mixture. Garnish with pimiento, if desired.

NOTE: Can be prepared a day in advance, covered and chilled.

PREPARATION TIME: 35 minutes (excluding chilling time)
YIELD: 16 egg halves

Snow Peas with Crabmeat Filling

The filling is also great in scooped out cherry tomatoes.

8   *ounces cream cheese*
1   *clove garlic, pressed*
1   *tablespoon grated onion*
2   *teaspoons coarse grain mustard*
1   *teaspoon lemon juice*
3   *tablespoons cooking sherry*
6   *ounces fresh crabmeat*
2   *tablespoons butter*
50-60 *snow peas*

1.   Melt cream cheese over low heat. Stir in the garlic, onion, mustard, lemon juice, and sherry.
2.   In a separate pan, sauté crabmeat for 3 minutes in 2 tablespoons butter. Stir the crab into the cream cheese mixture. Chill until firm but still spreadable.
3.   Remove stems and strings from snow peas.
4.   Blanch the peas in a large pot of boiling water for about 30 seconds and then immediately cover with cold water to preserve the bright green color. Drain well and slit open the straight seam of each snow pea.
5.   Pipe the crab mixture from a pastry bag or use a small spoon to fill each snow pea with some crabmeat filling.

PREPARATION TIME: 30 minutes (excluding chilling time)
YIELD: 50-60 hors d'ouevres

It has been said that the chief contribution of the Indians to the New England pioneers was the clambake. All along the Connecticut shoreline are found heaps of buried shells marking the old gathering places where the tribes assembled for their feasts of shellfish. The method of making the bake has remained unchanged from that which the Indians enjoyed.

Carleton Crabmeat Creation

This can be made a day ahead, covered and refrigerated.

½   cup mayonnaise
8   ounces cream cheese, softened
     juice of ½ lemon
1   tablespoon Worcestershire sauce
1   small onion, chopped fine
1   package frozen King Crab such as Wakefield
⅓   cup chili sauce
½   tablespoon prepared horseradish
     chopped parsley or chives

1. Blend together the mayonnaise, cream cheese, lemon juice, Worcestershire, and onion. Spread on the bottom of an elegant serving dish.
2. Sprinkle with crab to make a second layer.
3. Mix chili sauce and horseradish together and spread to make a third layer.
4. Sprinkle with parsley or chives to add color for the fourth layer.
5. Chill at least one hour before serving.

PREPARATION TIME: 20 minutes (excluding chilling time)
YIELD: 8-10 servings

King Charles II of England gave the early colonists of Connecticut a charter which allowed them to govern themselves without interference from the king. However, the next king, James II, tried to take back the charter. When the royal governor came to seize the charter, it had disappeared. The colonists had hidden it in the hollow of a huge oak tree in Hartford, nearly seven feet wide. The oak tree became the symbol of the peoples' freedom. The Charter Oak grew to be almost a thousand years old before it was blown down in 1856. A stone monument now marks the place where it stood.

Party Crab and Shrimp Spread

1	*6-ounce can crabmeat, picked over to remove shell bits*
1	*6-ounce can shrimp, drained of excess liquid*
2	*8-ounce packages cream cheese, softened*
1	*teaspoon lemon juice*
1	*tablespoon mayonnaise*
1	*small onion, chopped*
2	*tablespoons chili sauce*
2	*dashes Worcestershire sauce*
½	*cup chopped parsley*
½	*cup chopped pecans or walnuts*

1. Combine crab, shrimp, cream cheese, lemon juice, mayonnaise, onion, chili sauce and Worcestershire, mixing well to blend. Divide mixture in half and shape into two balls or mounds.
2. Combine parsley and chopped nuts. Sprinkle this mixture onto the rounds, pressing in evenly to coat. Wrap and refrigerate at least 2 hours. Bring back to room temperature before serving accompanied by crackers or party-size rye bread.

NOTE: One portion may be frozen for later use.

PREPARATION TIME: 20 minutes (excluding chilling time)
YIELD: 8-10 servings

Crabmeat Compo

One tester loved this recipe so much that now she always has some of these on hand in the freezer ready to go when unexpected company drops by.

1	*stick (8 tablespoons) butter, softened to room temperature*
1	*5-ounce jar Old English Cheddar cheese, room temperature*
1½	*teaspoons mayonnaise*
¼	*teaspoon garlic powder*

¼   teaspoon Lawry's seasoned salt
1   can crabmeat or ½ pound fresh crabmeat
6   whole English muffins

1. Combine softened butter and cheese in a mixing bowl with the mayonnaise, garlic powder, seasoned salt, and the crabmeat.
2. Split the muffins in half and spread some of the crabmeat mixture on each half. Arrange on a baking sheet and place in the freezer for 10 minutes or until firm enough to cut easily. Cut each muffin half into four or six bite-sized pieces. If not using immediately, freeze on baking sheet until solid, then bag carefully in plastic freezer bags and store for up to four weeks in the freezer.
3. Preheat broiler. Arrange on baking sheets and broil until bubbly and lightly browned. Serve warm.

PREPARATION TIME: 30 minutes
YIELD: 48-72 hors d'oeuvres

Crab and Cheese Dip

A family favorite for 24 years!

1   pound Velveeta cheese
¼   pound (8 tablespoons) butter
      Milk to thin, if needed
1   pound fresh lump crabmeat, picked over
6-8   drops Tabasco, or to taste
      Sherry to taste
      taco chips, Fritos or thinly sliced French bread

1. In top of double boiler, combine cheese and butter until melted. Add a little milk, if necessary to get a smooth consistency.
2. Add crabmeat, Tabasco and Sherry.
3. Serve hot, in chafing dish, with taco chips, Fritos, or thinly sliced French bread.

PREPARATION TIME: 15 minutes
YIELD: 12 servings

Gravlax with Mustard-Dill Sauce

3   *pounds fresh salmon, center cut*
1   *cup fresh dill sprigs*
¼   *cup kosher salt*
¼   *cup sugar*
1   *tablespoon white peppercorns*
1   *tablespoon black peppercorns*
     Mustard-Dill Sauce (recipe follows)

1. Ask the fish market to bone the salmon and to cut it in half lengthwise, leaving the skin on. Carefully check for any little bones, removing them with tweezers if you find any.
2. Place half the salmon, skin side down, in a glass dish long enough and deep enough to hold it and lay the dill on top of the fish. Combine the salt and sugar in a small bowl. Crush the white and black peppercorns using a mortar and pestle or wrap them in a towel and crush with the bottom of a heavy pan. Mix peppercorns with the salt and sugar and sprinkle this mixture over the fish. Lay the other half of the salmon, skin side up, over the seasoned fish. Cover first with plastic wrap, then with foil and weight the fish down with some large cans. Refrigerate for three days, turning every 12 hours or so and basting with the juices that are released.
3. Drain fish and pat dry. Lay skin side down, hold firmly with one hand and slice paper thin against the skin, leaving the skin behind as you make the slices. Serve slices on lightly buttered pumpernickel rounds topped with a small spoonful of Mustard-Dill Sauce.

PREPARATION TIME: 30 minutes
CURING: 3 days
YIELD: Enough for a large cocktail party or 10 at dinner

Mustard-Dill Sauce

8   *tablespoons Dijon mustard*
4   *teaspoons dry mustard*

6   *tablespoons sugar*
4   *tablespoons white wine vinegar*
1¼   *cups oil—half vegetable oil, half olive oil*
½   *cup chopped fresh dill*

1.   In a small deep bowl combine mustards, sugar and vinegar and mix until smooth. Using a wire whisk, beat oil into mixture, one drop at a time at the beginning and once it has begun to thicken, in a very thin stream. Sauce will resemble mayonnaise. Stir in fresh dill. Cover and refrigerate for as long as 2-3 days.

PREPARATION TIME: 15 minutes
YIELD: 1½ cups

★Smoked Salmon Paté

The nice smoky taste of the salmon provides the flavoring for this spread which comes from The Fisherman's Net in Darien.

¼   *pound smoked salmon*
2   *8-ounce packages cream cheese, softened*
6   *teaspoons minced onion*
4   *tablespoons fresh dill, chopped*
3   *tablespoons lemon juice*
¾   *teaspoon Tabasco*
    additional chopped dill and dill sprigs for garnish

1.   Chop the smoked salmon. Combine in a bowl with the cream cheese, onion, dill, lemon juice and Tabasco, mixing thoroughly with a wooden spoon or your hands to blend. Transfer to an attractive serving bowl, cover and refrigerate for at least 2 hours.
2.   To serve, sprinkle with additional chopped dill and garnish with dill sprigs. Spread on crackers or pumpernickel bread.

PREPARATION TIME: 15 minutes (excluding chilling time)
YIELD: 8-10 servings

Crab-Stuffed Snow Peas

A light and lovely hors d'oeuvre. Though somewhat painstaking to fill, the snow peas can be done as much as two hours before serving and held well-wrapped in the refrigerator.

1   *8-ounce package cream cheese, at room temperature*
1   *tablespoon lemon juice*
6   *ounces crabmeat, fresh or frozen*
2   *tablespoons finely chopped onion*
    salt and pepper to taste
8   *ounces snow peas (about 60), stems and strings removed*
1   *red pepper, seeded and cut in matchstick slivers*

1. In a bowl, beat cream cheese with the lemon juice until smooth. Add crabmeat and onion and mix well. Season to taste with salt and pepper. Cover and refrigerate for at least one hour until firm.
2. Bring a large pot of water to the boil. Blanch the snow peas for about 45 seconds. Remove with a slotted spoon and drop in a large bowl of very cold water to stop their cooking. Drain on paper towels and pat dry.
3. With the point of a sharp knife, split open the curved seam of each snow pea. Using a small spoon or knife, fill each snow pea with about 1½ teaspoons of the crabmeat mixture. Arrange on a serving platter and garnish with red pepper slivers.

PREPARATION TIME: 1-1½ hours (excluding chilling time)
YIELD: 60 stuffed snow peas

Scallop Blankets

Our testers thought this was a fabulous combination!

1	*pound sea scallops, cut into ½-inch cubes (24 pieces)*
4	*tablespoons sherry*
1	*teaspoon sugar*
1	*teaspoon salt*
12	*slices bacon, halved*
12	*water chestnuts, sliced*
2	*scallions, cut into 1 inch pieces*

1. Marinate the scallops in the sherry and sugar for at least 30 minutes. Sprinkle salt on scallops.
2. Preheat broiler.
3. Wrap a piece of bacon around a piece of scallop, a slice of water chestnut, and a piece of scallion. Secure with a toothpick.
4. Broil 4-5 inches from the heat source, turning once, for about 5 minutes until bacon crisps. Or, bake 10-12 minutes at 500 degrees.

PREPARATION TIME: 30 minutes (excluding marinating time)
YIELD: 24 pieces serving 8-12

Shrimp Marinated in Mustard Sauce

The sauce is delicately flavored so as not to overpower the shrimp.

2½   *pounds medium shrimp, peeled and deveined*
¼   *cup minced parsley*
¼   *cup chopped shallots*
¼   *cup tarragon vinegar*
½   *cup olive oil*
¼   *cup Dijon mustard*
2   *teaspoons red pepper flakes*
2   *teaspoons salt*
     fresh ground black pepper to taste

1.   Cook shrimp and drain. Place in a large bowl.
2.   Combine remaining ingredients and add to warm shrimp, being
     sure all shrimp are well coated.
3.   Cover and refrigerate at least one hour.
4.   Serve with toothpicks.

PREPARATION TIME: 20 minutes (excluding chilling time)
YIELD: 10-12 servings

*Stonington had a "character" of sorts named "Uncle" Zebbie Hancox who
became a recluse after being spurned in love because he had no money. He
lived in a shack and earned money doing menial jobs on the wharves,
fishing, and building homes. He never spent a dime and even whittled his
own buttons. Local boys played tricks on him by dropping dead fish down
his chimney. He died in 1899 at the age of 91 leaving an estate worth
$100,000 and fourteen houses on Hancox Street which still bears his name.*

Shrimp Mousse

Easy to make, great for a party. It looks pretty and tastes good!

1   envelope Knox gelatin
¼   cup cold water
1   8-ounce package cream cheese, softened
1   can tomato soup
1   cup mayonnaise
1   pound cooked shrimp, chopped
½   cup chopped onion
½   cup chopped celery

1.   Prepare a 1½-quart mold by lining with plastic wrap, pressing it in as smoothly as you can with your hands.
2.   Sprinkle gelatin over cold water and set aside for 5 minutes to soften.
3.   Whisk together the cream cheese and tomato soup until smooth—or do this in the food processor. Transfer to a medium saucepan, stir in the softened gelatin and stir gently over low heat until warm—do not boil. Remove from heat and add mayonnaise, shrimp, onion and celery and stir until well combined. Pour mousse mixture into prepared mold, cover with plastic wrap and refrigerate until firm, at least 3 hours.
4.   Invert onto a serving platter, peel off plastic wrap and surround with crackers.

NOTE: Shrimp, onion and celery may be chopped in the food processor.

PREPARATION TIME: 20 minutes (excluding chilling time)
YIELD: 8-12 servings

★Tom's Shrimp Taco

Very colorful and pretty on an hors d'oeuvres table.

8   *ounces cream cheese, softened*
¼   *cup whipping cream*
½   *bottle chili sauce*
4   *ounce can cooked tiny shrimp, drained, rinsed and dried well*
6   *scallions, chopped*
¾   *green pepper, chopped*
1   *small can (3-4 ounces) pitted black olives, drained, dried with a*
      paper towel and sliced
1   *large package (8 ounces) grated mozzarella cheese*
      plain round Doritos

1. Mix cream cheese and whipping cream. Pat down on a platter.
2. Spread remaining ingredients in order that they appear. Chill at least one hour before serving.
3. Serve with Doritos.

NOTE: This can be made a day ahead provided that shrimp and olives are well-drained and patted dry.

PREPARATION TIME: 30 minutes (excluding chilling time)
YIELD: 8 servings

In 1785, during a time of prohibition, James Rhodes purchased a small island off of Stonington with the intent of selling liquor to sailors. The state lines of Connecticut, Rhode Island, and New York were said to meet on the island. He constructed a large saloon where the three state lines came together. When prohibition agents from one state entered, the sailors quickly moved to the other side of the room where agents had no authority to arrest them. Today, the island is known as Rhodes Folly.

Shrimp Butter

Simply super and very easy to prepare. A decorative presentation is to spoon the Shrimp Butter into a hollowed out green pepper.

1	*7-ounce can shrimp, drained*
1	*stick (8 tablespoons) butter, at room temperature*
1	*small container (8-ounce) whipped cream cheese, at room temperature*
1	*tablespoon mayonnaise*
½	*cup finely chopped green pepper*
½	*cup finely chopped green onion*
⅓	*cup finely chopped celery*
½	*teaspoon dried minced onion*
½	*teaspoon white pepper*
	salt to taste
	raw vegetables or crackers

1. In a medium bowl, mix all ingredients except raw vegetables or crackers. Add salt to taste at the end. Chill until spreadable.
2. Serve with the vegetables or crackers.

PREPARATION TIME: 20 minutes (excluding chilling time)
YIELD: 8-12 servings

Shrimp Elégant

If you use lobster, this is even more "elegant"!

1	*tablespoon unflavored gelatin*
¼	*cup cold water*
1	*can (10¾ ounces) condensed tomato soup*
3	*ounces cream cheese*
½	*cup finely chopped celery*
½	*cup finely chopped onion*
½	*cup finely chopped green pepper*
2	*tablespoons Worcestershire sauce*
1	*cup mayonnaise*
1	*cup cooked fresh medium shrimp or 4½-ounce can medium shrimp, drained*
	crackers for spreading

1. Lightly oil a 6-cup mold.
2. Soften gelatin in the cold water.
3. Melt the soup and cheese together over low heat.
4. Pour the soup mixture into a mixing bowl, add the gelatin and beat until smooth. Stir in the remaining ingredients and pour into the mold. Refrigerate until firm, at least 3 hours
5. Serve with crackers for cocktails.

PREPARATION TIME: 30 minutes (excluding chilling time)
YIELD: 12-15 servings

One of the laws regulating oysters prohibited their taking during the months without an "R". Although this was done as a conservation measure during spawning, people erroneously came to believe that oysters were inedible in May, June, July, and August.

Tuna Mold Pawcatuck

1   *envelope unflavored gelatin*
¼   *cup hot water*
1   *medium onion*
⅔   *cup cottage cheese*
⅓   *cup sour cream*
½   *cup mayonnaise*
2   *7-ounce cans white water-packed tuna, drained*
     juice of 1 lemon
1   *teaspoon dried dill weed*

1. Sprinkle gelatin into hot water and stir occasionally until dissolved.
2. Cut the onion in quarters and chop in a food processor. Add all remaining ingredients and process until smooth. Turn into a bowl and stir in dissolved gelatin until well blended.
3. Line a 1-quart mold with plastic wrap, pressing it in as smoothly as possible with your hands. Pour tuna mixture into mold, cover, and refrigerate until set, at least 2 hours. Invert onto a serving platter, peel off plastic wrap, surround with crackers and serve.

PREPARATION TIME: 15 minutes (excluding chilling time)
YIELD: 8 servings

Coastal waters have provided many riches, including our first "currency". Wampum was cut into tubular beads and came in two forms. Black wampum, the more valuable, was cut from the shells of clams and mussels. White wampum came from the inside of the conch shell. Crafty white settlers eventually employed Indians to produce counterfeit wampum by dyeing the white beads black.

★Curried Tuna in Endive Sheaves

A very sophisticated tuna hors d'oeuvres from the Soho Charcuterie Restaurant in Manhattan. It is also good spread on black bread toast rounds.

½   *cup finely diced apple*
¼   *cup finely diced celery*
1   *packed tablespoon currants*
¾   *cup scallions, sliced in ¼ inch rounds*
1   *tablespoon minced red onion*
2   *level tablespoons blanched, sliced, toasted almonds*
1   *(7½-ounce) can solid or chunk tuna in water, drained*
     Curried Mayonnaise (recipe follows)
2   *large Belgian endive*

1. Combine all ingredients except tuna, mayonnaise and endive in a mixing bowl.
2. Add tuna and enough mayonnaise to bind. Stir well, and chill at least one hour.
3. Separate the leaves of endive and wash each in cold water. Drain and dry well on paper toweling.
4. Just before serving, spoon about a tablespoon of the tuna mixture into the hollows of the endive spears and arrange on a platter.

PREPARATION TIME: 30 minutes (excluding chilling time)
YIELD: 8-10 servings

Yankee whaling crews sailing to the Azores signed on Portuguese who returned to Stonington and prospered as commercial fishermen. Today, Stonington's commercial fishing fleet has crews who come from a thriving Portuguese enclave with its own ethnic flavor.

Curried Mayonnaise

1   *egg*
2   *egg yolks*
¼   *cup curry powder*
1½   *tablespoons chutney*
1½   *tablespoons tarragon vinegar*
1   *teaspoon freshly squeezed lemon juice*
¼   *teaspoon salt, optional*
¼   *teaspoon freshly ground black pepper*
1¾   *cup light vegetable oil, approximately*

1. Place all ingredients except oil in a food processor or mixing bowl. (If mixing by hand, chop the chutney in small pieces.)
2. Process or whisk while very very slowly dribbling the oil to reach desired mayonnaise consistency. Taste and adjust salt and pepper.

PREPARATION TIME: 15 minutes
YIELD: about 2 cups

New London and Groton

The sea has always been a life-giving force to New London, and generations of New Londoners have made everlasting contributions to the seas. Situated at the mouth of the Thames River, New London and Groton were blessed with waters that formed the largest and deepest harbor on the Connecticut coastline. From its earliest beginnings, maritime commerce was its lifeblood, first with shipbuilding and later with the daring exploits of its seamen.

It was during the American Revolution, after all, that New London became a virtual hornets' nest of privateers, brave seamen who preyed on the insidious British blockade. So hurtful was their sting that turncoat Benedict Arnold was sent to destroy the town.

The whaling era was the real heyday when New London achieved international fame. Although whales had been hunted in local waters as early as the 17th century, it was not until 1820 that whaling became serious business. It reached its peak in 1847 when New London as a whaling port ranked third behind New Bedford and Nantucket. Whaling was more than a statistic; it was a way of life with most of the town's population connected in one way or another to a related industry. Wharves bustled with activity, and an international community settled in. New London became a very wealthy port, and as a result launched some of the country's first banking institutions. The glory days began to fade, however, when oil was discovered in Pennsylvania. The Civil War brought further decline as whalers were subjected to raids, even in distant waters. There were fewer whales at this point, and voyages to hunt them became longer and more expensive to equip. By the end of the 19th century, no whaling craft sailed out of the New London harbor.

There is little to show of this era except for a few Greek revival homes of sea captains on Whale Row where one can visit the Tale of the Whale Museum. Nevertheless, New London is still an industrious port and maritime center. It is home to the Coast Guard

APPETIZERS

New London Lighthouse

Academy and to the Naval Underwater System Center which develops sonar systems for submarines. Groton is called the submarine capital of the free world, for it is the site of the Naval submarine base and school. Local industry there has also been producing more than half of this country's submarine fleet since 1900, including the Nautilus, the first atomic submarine.

It almost goes without saying that this is a place where there's a connection between man and his environment. Whether they're atop of the waves or moving below their surfaces, New Londoners' bond with the sea is evident. It is a bond that goes beyond livelihood; it is in their souls.

★Volcano Clams

A really unusual appetizer that is a show stopper every time! It's one that the contributor acquired from the Australian Embassy when she was living in Seoul, Korea. Yes, the lemon extract really does ignite, but as with any flambéing, just be sure to avert your face when lighting it.

24	*cherrystone clams*
4	*whole water chestnuts*
¼	*cup bean sprouts, rinsed, drained and chopped*
2	*scallions, minced*
2	*teaspoons soy sauce*
½	*teaspoon grated fresh ginger*
2	*tablespoons butter*
2	*tablespoons flour*
½	*teaspoon salt*
⅛	*teaspoon pepper*
1	*cup light cream*
¼	*cup grated Parmesan cheese*
2	*tablespoons sesame seeds*
4	*tablespoons lemon extract*
	rock salt or kosher salt and sand (about 3 cups of each) for baking dishes

1. Remove clams from shells. (Have the fish market do this if possible.) Reserve 24 clean shells.

2. Dice clams and water chestnuts and combine with bean sprouts, scallion, soy sauce and ginger. Divide this mixture equally among the 24 shells.

3. In a medium saucepan, melt butter. Stir in flour, salt and pepper and cook over medium heat for 2 minutes. Slowly stir in the cream and cook for another two minutes, stirring constantly until very thick. Remove from heat and stir in the cheese. Spoon sauce

over clams. Recipe can be prepared ahead to this point. Cover and refrigerate for up to 6 hours. Bring back to room temperature before baking.

4. Preheat oven to 450 degrees. Mix together the salt and sand and make a one-inch layer in two large baking dishes. Set clams firmly in the bed of sand and salt making sure the shells do not overlap. Sprinkle clams with the sesame seeds and bake in the preheated oven for 6 minutes.

5. Bring baking dishes to the table. Pour lemon extract over clams and between them onto the salt/sand mixture. Dim the lights and ignite for a stunning effect. Allow guests to help themselves.

PREPARATION TIME: 45 minutes
COOKING TIME: 6 minutes
YIELD: 24 clams (6 servings)

Clams Casino

12 *medium Little Neck clams*
¼ *cup finely chopped onion*
¼ *cup finely chopped green pepper*
¼ *cup finely chopped celery*
2 *slices bacon*
2 *tablespoons minced parsley*
lemon wedges

1. Open clams and leave them on the half shell.
2. Sprinkle onion, green pepper and celery on each. Top with a 1-inch strip of bacon and sprinkle with parsley.
3. Place under broiler until bacon is crispy.
4. Serve with lemon wedges.

NOTE: Clams are easier to open if placed in the freezer for several minutes prior to opening.

PREPARATION TIME: 15 minutes
YIELD: 3-4 servings

Baked Stuffed Clams

A real New England specialty.

24 *small hard-shell clams such as Cherrystone (have the fishmonger*
    open and place them on the half shell)
2   *tablespoons lemon juice*
¼   *cup freshly grated Parmesan cheese*
¼   *cup seasoned bread crumbs*
¼   *cup finely chopped parsley*
2   *cloves garlic, crushed*
1   *teaspoon oregano*
½   *teaspoon salt*
    freshly ground black pepper
    olive oil
    lemon slices

1. Preheat oven to 425 degrees. Arrange the clams in a single layer
    in a shallow baking dish. Sprinkle each clam with a little lemon
    juice.
2. Combine the cheese, bread crumbs, parsley, garlic, oregano,
    salt, and pepper. Spoon about 1 teaspoon of this mixture over
    each clam. Put a drop of olive oil on each clam.
3. Bake about 15 minutes until browned. Serve with lemon slices.

NOTE: If you must open the clams yourself, put them on a baking
sheet and heat in oven 4-5 minutes until they open. Or place in the
freezer for a few minutes which makes them easier to open with a
knife.

PREPARATION TIME: 20 minutes
YIELD: 4-6 servings

Because of poor pay, it was difficult to recruit whaling crews, so little or no
experience was required. A common way for a criminal to escape the law was
to sign on for an extended whaling voyage.

Moules Ravigote

6   *dozen mussels*
1   *cup mayonnaise*
2   *teaspoons lemon juice*
¼   *cup capers, drained*
2   *cloves minced garlic*
1   *bunch scallions, chopped coarsely*
¼   *cup parsley, chopped fine*
     paprika for garnish

1. Wash and debeard the mussels. Steam in about 3 cups water over low flame until they open, 5-10 minutes. Let cool until you can handle them.
2. Combine remaining ingredients except paprika in a bowl.
3. Chop 18 of the mussels and add to the ingredients in the bowl.
4. Remove the top shell from the remaining mussels and arrange them, on the half-shell, on a large platter or on separate serving plates.
5. Place a spoonful of sauce on top of each mussel. Sprinkle with paprika. Serve chilled or at room temperature.

PREPARATION TIME: 45 minutes
YIELD: 4½ dozen mussels

Although whaling made ports such as New London very wealthy, a voyage for the common seaman was not very profitable. The owners of the ship usually took two-thirds of the profits. Out of the remainder, the captain and first mate each received ¹/₈, the cook ¹/₁₀₀, and the common seaman ¹/₁₅₀. After monies for extra expenses such as clothing and tobacco were deducted, it was possible for the seaman to owe money and, thus, have to sign on for another voyage to pay off the debt.

Lobster Quesadillas

This recipe first appeared in Melanie Barnard's COOK'S Magazine column titled "Quick From Scratch."

2	*1-1½ pound lobsters*
8	*large flour tortillas*
1	*jalapeno pepper, fresh or canned*
1	*large tomato, peeled and seeded*
1	*small onion*
1	*canned mild green poblano chile or ½ green bell pepper*
4	*sprigs cilantro*
	salt and pepper to taste
4	*tablespoons butter*
3-4	*scallions, thinly sliced, including one inch of green part*
4	*ounces snow peas, trimmed and cut in half on the diagonal*
1	*ripe avocado, peeled and cut in bite sized chunks*
¼	*teaspoon cumin*
1	*tablespoon lime juice*
½	*cup sour cream*
	additional cilantro sprigs for garnish

1. Preheat oven to 300 degrees. Bring a pot of water large enough to hold the lobsters to a boil. Plunge lobsters, head first, into the rapidly boiling water, cover pot and bring back to a boil. Uncover and boil about 12 minutes until lobsters are cooked. Remove from pot and when cool enough to handle, remove meat from tail and claws. Cut meat into bite size pieces. (Alternatively, twelve ounces purchased cooked lobster meat may be used).

2. While lobsters are cooking, wrap the tortillas in foil and warm in the preheated oven for about 15 minutes.

3. Remove seeds and ribs from the jalapeno pepper (wear gloves if desired to protect the hands from the hot pepper). Place pep-

per, tomato, onion, poblano chile and cilantro in a food processor and chop. Season the salsa with salt and pepper and set aside.

4. In a medium skillet, heat the butter and sauté the scallions and
    snow peas over medium-high heat for about 2 minutes. Add the
    avocado, cumin, lime juice and salt and pepper to taste. Add the
    lobster meat and cook, tossing, about 30 seconds until warmed
    through. Spoon the filling over the bottom half of the warmed
    tortillas and fold over.

5. Serve the quesadillas garnished with spoonfuls of the salsa and
    sour cream. Decorate each plate with additional cilantro sprigs.

PREPARATION AND COOKING TIME: 45 minutes
YIELD: Serves 8 for a first course
         Serves 4 for a main course

Crabmeat Shells "Au Groton"

A super-simple appetizer.

1   cup crabmeat
2   tablespoons finely chopped onion
½   cup mayonnaise
8   ounces cream cheese, softened
1   egg, beaten

1. Blend all ingredients and beat until fluffy.
2. Divide among 4-6 scallop-shaped or other individual ramekins.
    Bake 20-25 minutes at 350 degrees until puffed and brown.

PREPARATION TIME: 10 minutes
BAKING TIME: 20-25 minutes
YIELD: 4-6 servings

Moules de la Block

A lovely neat way to present mussels as an appetizer or hors d'oeuvre—
and the recipe can be prepared ahead of time.

2	*dozen fresh mussels*
¼	*cup dry mustard*
8	*tablespoons (1 stick) butter, softened*
1	*medium onion, finely chopped*
1	*large clove garlic, minced*
½	*cup seasoned fine dry Italian bread crumbs, such as Progresso*
¼	*cup minced parsley*
	salt and black pepper to taste

1. Scrub mussels, pull off their beards and soak in 1 quart of water to which ¼ cup dry mustard has been added for 30 minutes. Drain and rinse in cold water.
2. Place mussels in a large kettle or steamer with 2 cups of fresh water. Bring to a boil, cover and cook over medium-high heat for 5-8 minutes or just until their shells open. Remove from heat, drain, and when cool enough to handle, break off and discard top shell of each mussel. Arrange mussels in a 9 x 13″ broiler pan or baking sheet and set aside.
3. In a small bowl mix together the softened butter, onion, garlic, bread crumbs, parsley and salt and pepper. (Vegetables may be chopped in food processor and butter mixture combined in bowl of processor if desired.) Spread a generous amount of butter over each mussel. Recipe may be prepared up to several hours in advance to this point. Cover and refrigerate.
4. Preheat broiler. Place mussels under broiler approximately 5 inches from the heat source and cook for 5 minutes or until lightly browned and bubbly. Transfer to a platter and garnish with parsley if desired.

PREPARATION TIME: 45 minutes
COOKING TIME: 5 minutes
YIELD: 4-5 appetizer servings

Bloody Mary Oysters

This recipe came originally from the Maryland shore.

3 *dozen oysters on the half shell*
¾ *cup prepared chili sauce, such as Heinz*
  juice of half a lemon
1 *tablespoon Worcestershire sauce*
2 *teaspoons horseradish*
  Tabasco sauce to taste (the spicier the better)
  salt and freshly ground pepper to taste

1. Open the oysters or have the fish market do this for you. Arrange on a bed of cracked ice.
2. Mix remaining ingredients for sauce.
3. Serve sauce with oysters on small plates with fish forks or let guests help themselves with fingers and provide lots of cocktail napkins.

NOTE: Sauce will keep well in refrigerator for up to two weeks.

PREPARATION TIME: 10 minutes—if fish market opens oysters
YIELD: 6-8 servings

During the War of 1812, numerous maritime skirmishes occurred in coastal Connecticut waters. In one such event, volunteers preparing the cannons at Fort Griswold against an impending British attack discovered a shortage of gun wadding. A search party went out to nearby homes in Groton requesting flannel to use to wad their cannons. Mrs. Anna Bailey made a donation of cloth: she dropped her red flannel petticoat to her feet and exclaimed, "Give this to the British at the cannon's mouth." Over the years, "Mother Bailey" was paid respect by President Monroe, General Lafayette, and President Andrew Jackson for her patriotism.

Salmon Timbales with
Watercress Sauce

An elegant appetizer for a special dinner party.

Timbales:

1   *pound boneless and skinless fresh salmon, cut in 1-inch cubes*
4   *large eggs*
1   *teaspoon grated onion*
3-4   *drops Tabasco*
1½   *teaspoons salt*
½   *teaspoon pepper*
1½   *cups heavy cream, well-chilled*

Sauce:

8   *bunches watercress*
1   *tablespoon lemon juice*
12   *tablespoons unsalted butter*
½   *cup heavy cream*
½   *cup milk*
       salt and freshly ground pepper to taste
       watercress sprigs for garnish

1. Preheat oven to 375 degrees. Grease a muffin pan for one dozen
    muffins.
2. To make the timbales, place the salmon in a food processor and
    pulse on and off until coarsely chopped. Add eggs, grated onion,
    Tabasco, salt and pepper to the workbowl and process until
    smooth, about one minute. Scrape down bowl once or twice.

With the motor running, slowly pour cream through feed tube. Stop machine, scrape down sides of bowl and process for another 10 seconds.

3. Bring a kettle of water to the boil for the water bath. Divide salmon mixture equally among the 12 muffin cups, set the muffin tin in a large baking dish and pour in enough boiling water to come halfway up the sides. Bake 12-15 minutes until timbales are set and a toothpick inserted in the center comes out clean.

4. To make the sauce, bring a large pot of water to the boil. Pick over watercress, removing tough stems, and rinse under running water. Salt the water, and when it has come to a rapid boil, blanch the watercress for 3 minutes. Drain into a colander and plunge immediately into cold water to stop the cooking and set the color. Squeeze out as much water as possible. (Watercress may be prepared up to 4 hours ahead to this point. Store well-covered in the refrigerator.)

5. Puree the watercress in a food processor, scraping down sides twice. Place puree in a saucepan and add lemon juice, butter, cream and milk. Heat gently, stirring with a wooden spoon until smooth. Add salt and pepper to taste.

6. To serve, spoon a pool of sauce onto each of 12 warm plates, place one timbale on the sauce, and garnish with a sprig of watercress.

PREPARATION AND COOKING TIME: 1 hour
YIELD: 12 servings

Scallops with Shallot Butter and Pine Nuts

Serve this elegant and unusual scallop dish as a first course preceding a company dinner of roast lamb or beef.

1	*pound scallops*
12	*tablespoons butter, softened*
3	*tablespoons finely chopped shallots*
	salt to taste
2	*tablespoons coarsely chopped pine nuts*
1	*tablespoon chopped parsley*
⅓	*cup fine dry bread crumbs*
1	*tablespoon lemon juice*

1. Preheat oven to 500 degrees. Rinse scallops and pat dry.
2. In a small bowl, combine butter, shallots, salt, pine nuts, parsley, bread crumbs and lemon juice. Work together with a wooden spoon or with fingers until well mixed. Divide the scallops in equal amounts among 6 scallop shells or small ramekins. Dot with equal portions of the butter. Place on a baking sheet and bake in the preheated oven for 10 minutes or until brown and bubbly. Place each ramekin on a plate for serving.

PREPARATION TIME: 15 minutes
COOKING TIME: 10 minutes
YIELD: 6 first course servings

In colonial days, salmon and shad were not the delicacies they are today. Apprentices and farm help would often designate in their work contracts that salmon would only be served twice a week. The same held true for shad which was considered "poor men's food" and sometimes used as fertilizer.

Coquille St. Jacques

One-half pound shrimp can be substituted for either the scallops or crabmeat if you wish.

⅓   *cup minced onion*
1   *clove minced garlic*
⅓   *cup unsalted butter*
¼   *cup flour*
½   *teaspoon salt*
¼   *teaspoon pepper*
1⅓   *cup milk*
⅔   *cup Sauternes or other white wine*
1   *pound bay scallops*
7½   *ounces crabmeat*
     grated Parmesan cheese

1. Sauté the onion and garlic in the butter over medium-low heat until softened. Remove from heat and blend in flour, salt and pepper. Return to heat and stir until bubbly. Remove from heat and stir in milk and wine. Heat to a boil, stirring constantly, and then cook, stirring, for one minute.
2. Add scallops and crabmeat and cook, stirring, for one minute.
3. Spoon into 6-8 individual small scallop or other shape ramekins. Sprinkle top with cheese.
4. Broil 6-8 inches from the heat source for 2-4 minutes until bubbly and lightly browned.

NOTE: This can be prepared in the morning and refrigerated. Let stand at room temperature before filling the shells.
PREPARATION TIME: 45 minutes
YIELD: 6-8 servings

Martha Stewart's Seafood Sausage with Lemon Herb Butter

From cookbook author and entertainer par excellence, Martha Stewart.

For the seafood sausage:

1   *pound sole fillets, cut into pieces*
1   *pound salmon steak, skinned, boned, chopped coarse*
½   *pound raw shrimp, peeled, deveined and chopped coarse*
4   *large eggs*
½   *cup heavy cream*
½   *teaspoon salt*
½   *teaspoon white pepper*
2   *teaspoons minced fresh parsley*

For the sauce:

½   *cup dry white wine*
2   *tablespoons fresh lemon juice*
2   *teaspoons white wine vinegar*
2   *sticks (16 tablespoons) unsalted butter, cut into bits*
1   *teaspoon freshly grated lemon rind*
2   *teaspoons minced scallion*
2   *teaspoons minced fresh parsley*
2   *teaspoons snipped fresh dill*
      cayenne pepper to taste

For the garnish:

8   *cooked shrimp, shelled, leaving the tails intact*
      shredded scallion green, soaked in cold water for 5 minutes and
      then patted dry

1.   To make the seafood sausage, puree the sole in a food processor, scraping down the sides of the bowl several times. Remove puree

to a mixing bowl and chill 30 minutes. In another bowl, chill the salmon and shrimp, covered for 1½ hours.

2. In the food processor, blend the sole puree, eggs, cream, salt, and pepper until well-blended. Transfer back to the mixing bowl and chill, covered, for 1 hour. Fold the sole puree, eggs, shrimp, salmon and parsley together. Divide the mixture between 2 (12 inch) square sheets of Saran wrap and form the mixture into 2 logs using the Saran wrap to roll and shape. Twist the ends of the Saran wrap securely.

3. Wrap each sausage in foil and poach in a large kettle of simmering water for 10-15 minutes until a metal skewer inserted into the center comes out hot. Transfer the sausages to a cutting board and let stand for 10 minutes.

4. To make the sauce, boil the wine, lemon juice and vinegar in a heavy saucepan until reduced by half. Reduce heat to very low and whisk in the butter, bit by bit, lifting the pan from the heat occasionally to keep the butter from liquefying. Whisk in the lemon rind, scallion, parsley, dill, cayenne, and salt to taste.

5. To serve, pour the sauce onto a platter, unwrap sausages and cut into ¾-inch slices and arrange over the sauce. Garnish with shrimp and scallion greens.

PREPARATION TIME: 1 hour (excluding refrigerating time)
COOKING TIME: 15 minutes
YIELD: 8 first course servings

Almost every Saturday in May, there is a "Shad Plank" fish bake in either Old Saybrook or Essex. Shad fillets caught the night before are affixed to thick oak planks, held in place by nailed strips of salt pork. The planks are then set upright in a circle surrounding an open oak bonfire, with the shad fillets facing inward toward the heat. The best part, of course, is standing around watching the fire and talking to the old-time shad fishermen who run it!

Scallop and Salmon Terrine

This is especially nice served with mayonnaise seasoned with lemon juice
and minced watercress.

	juice of one lemon
½	*cup white wine*
	scant 2 tablespoons chopped fresh tarragon
1¾	*teaspoons salt*
1	*teaspoon fresh ground pepper (preferably white pepper)*
¾	*pound salmon fillet, boned, skinned and cut into ¼-inch strips*
½	*cup diced carrots*
1	*shallot, minced*
1½	*tablespoons butter*
8	*fresh asparagus spears*
1½	*pounds fresh spinach, cleaned and without stems*
¾	*pound scallops (see note)*
1	*egg*
	scant ¼ teaspoon cayenne pepper
1¾	*cup heavy cream*

1. Combine lemon juice, wine, 1 tablespoon of the tarragon, ¾ teaspoon of the salt, ½ teaspoon pepper, and salmon. Marinate 3 hours in the refrigerator.
2. Sauté the carrots and shallots in the butter for about 10 minutes over medium-low heat until softened.
3. Cook the asparagus in boiling salted water for about 3 minutes until crisp-tender. Drain under cold water to stop the cooking.
4. Blanch or steam the spinach for less than a minute in ½ cup water. Drain. Try to keep the leaves whole.
5. Preheat oven to 350 degrees. Butter a 5-cup loaf pan.
6. In a food processor, purée the scallops, 1 tablespoon tarragon, 1 teaspoon salt, ½ teaspoon pepper, and cayenne until smooth. Slowly add the cream through the feed tube until blended.

7. Combine the carrot mixture and the scallops.

8. Make a ¼-½ inch layer of spinach on the bottom of the prepared pan. Drape largest and most intact leaves over sides of pan to form a complete cover. Reserve remaining leaves for the top of the terrine.

9. Make a 1-inch layer of scallop mousse and then layer on 4 of the asparagus spears. Fill in spaces between the asparagus with more mousse.

10. Lay salmon lengthwise over the asparagus. Add a thin layer of mousse and arrange the remaining asparagus over this. Fill pan with remaining mousse.

11. Fold spinach leaves over top of mousse and fill in any gaps with reserved spinach.

12. Butter a piece of aluminum foil and put on top of the terrine, buttered side down. Place the pan in a larger pan half-filled with hot water. Bake 1 hour and 15 minutes until firm to the touch. (Do not let water in pan boil.)

13. Remove from oven and cool completely. Refrigerate for at least 24 hours. Before unmolding, tip pan so that any excess liquid can drain off. Unmold and serve cut into slices.

NOTE: Sea scallops are preferred for their snowy white color.

PREPARATION TIME: 1½ hours (excluding marinating time)
BAKING TIME: 1 hour and 15 minutes
YIELD: 12 servings

Connecticut River shad roe is considered to be among the world's best. The colder water of the Connecticut River forces the shad to start spawning almost a month later which accounts for the fuller, firmer and more flavorsome roe. The shad lives in the ocean but returns to fresh water estuaries to spawn. The roe is the egg sack, two in each hen shad. On the Connecticut, an estimated six million shad run annually. They are caught at night in drift nets, the shad swimming up stream while two shad boats, with their weighted nets strung between them, ride the current down river.

Shrimp with Sun-Dried Tomatoes and Chevre

Here is an adaptation of a Craig Claiborne recipe that was printed in *The New York Times* two or three years ago. When one of our testers served this at a dinner party it got rave reviews!

1½   *pounds large shrimp*
¼   *pound sun-dried tomatoes packed in oil*
3   *tablespoons extra-virgin olive oil or light olive oil such as Sasso*
3   *medium cloves garlic, minced*
4   *teaspoons drained capers*
½   *teaspoon oregano*
½-⅔   *cup crumbled goat cheese such as Montrachet*

1. Shell and devein shrimp. Finely chop the tomatoes, reserving the oil. (Since sun-dried tomatoes are sometimes quite tough, chop on a sturdy cutting board using a good large sharp knife.) In a small bowl combine the tomatoes, reserved packing oil, additional olive oil, garlic, capers and oregano. Add shrimp and toss to coat well with sauce.
2. Divide shrimp mixture equally among 8 individual ramekins (for appetizer portions) or 9 x 13″ baking dish (for main course). Sprinkle shrimp evenly with goat cheese. Recipe may be made several hours ahead to this point and kept covered in the refrigerator.
3. Preheat oven to 450 degrees. Bake for 15-18 minutes or until shrimp turn pink and opaque. Place ramekins on plates and present as a first course or spoon over pasta as a main course.

PREPARATION TIME: 30 minutes
COOKING TIME: 15-18 minutes
YIELD: 8 servings as appetizer
4-6 as entree

★Scallop Ceviche

Bread and butter make a good accompaniment.

2   *pounds bay scallops*
1   *cup fresh lime juice*
¼   *cup chopped parsley*
½   *cup chopped scallions*
½   *cup chopped green pepper*
½   *cup chopped red pepper*
½   *cup olive oil*
1   *tablespoon chopped fresh basil or 1 teaspoon dried basil*
      salt and pepper to taste
      Boston lettuce leaves

1. Marinate scallops in the lime juice overnight to "cook" them. Stir occasionally to make sure scallops are evenly coated with the lime juice.
2. Drain and discard lime juice. Add remaining ingredients to scallops and mix thoroughly. Serve each portion on a leaf of Boston lettuce.

PREPARATION TIME: 30 minutes (excluding marinating time)
YIELD: 8 servings

"Scampi" Bluff Point

To say that all the tests on this one were enthusiastically received is an understatement. "I want this recipe *now!*" and "Don't change a thing!" were a couple of the comments.

1¼   *pounds large shrimp*
½   *cup olive oil*
2   *teaspoons chopped garlic*
2   *tablespoons chopped parsley*
⅛   *teaspoon dried red pepper flakes*
½   *teaspoon oregano*
3   *tablespoons fine fresh bread crumbs*
     salt and pepper to taste

1.   Preheat broiler. Shell and devein shrimp. Combine all other ingredients in a bowl, add the shrimp and toss to coat evenly.

2.   Arrange shrimp in a single layer in a broiler pan or rimmed baking sheet. Position 3-4 inches beneath broiling element and cook for 5-6 minutes until shrimp have turned pink and are lightly browned on the edges. Baste with some of the sauce in the pan and serve. Divide among individual plates as an appetizer or serve from a platter with toothpicks as an hors d'oeuvre.

PREPARATION TIME: 20 minutes
COOKING TIME: 5 minutes
YIELD: 4-6 servings

Ernie, the ghost of New London Ledge Lighthouse, was once a keeper of the light, but he threw himself into the water after his wife ran off with a ferry boat captain.

Connecticut River Valley

Around the area where the Connecticut River flows into the Long Island Sound are some of the most charming and picturesque towns in the state. Architecture speaks softly of a bygone era when shipping and shipbuilding were lively enterprises. Quaint cottages are reminders of the late nineteenth century when the area first became popular as a seaside resort. Time marches a little more slowly in this place where the past blends gently with the present. A lovely mellow and tranquil quality lingers here and continues to attract, for in the summer the population doubles in size with visitors beckoned by the yachting, boating, marinas, fishing, and beaches.

In East Lyme, the Chamber of Commerce sponsors the Annual Bluefish Tournament which lasts from August to October. The town also serves up delicious Niantic Bay Scallops for which they are known. Boaters and yachtsmen alike explore the coves and inlets around Lyme which is steeped in unspoiled rural beauty. Old Lyme, on the other hand, has long been a cultural and artistic center, with landscapes that featured prominently in the paintings of the American Impressionists.

East Haddam is most famous for its Goodspeed Opera House, a magnificent example of wooden Victorian architecture and certainly one of the prettiest small theatres in America. When it was built in 1876, its owner, William Goodspeed spared no expense transporting shows for one night stands from New York. Saved from demolition and renovated in 1963, the Goodspeed is still much alive, having premiered such shows as "Man of La Mancha," "Shenandoah," and "Annie".

Also along this estuary is a town whose spirit and community life have always been happily wedded to its surroundings. That town is Essex, a town whose essential character comes from the river. In its earliest days, Essex was a major distribution point for the West Indies trade. Later, trade with Zanzibar brought ivory from which the first combs were made. Piano keys are still manufactured in nearby Ivoryton, so named for this valued import.

Shipbuilding was always important. It was the shipyards of Essex, after all, that produced the *Oliver Cromwell*, the first ship of the colonial navy to go to sea. So prolific were these shipyards that the

SOUPS AND CHOWDERS

ESSEX, CT.

British raided Essex during the War of 1812, destroying twenty-two vessels. Scenes of this battle are the subject of murals in the dining room of the Griswold Inn (the "Gris"), a popular dining spot.

Shipbuilding continues today in this celebrated yachting center and quintessential New England town. While charming shops lure the tourist, venerable old colonial and federal houses stand on tree-lined streets, framed by the serene beauty of the river.

At the very mouth of the Connecticut River is one of the oldest settlements in the state, Old Saybrook. It was originally established to attract the elite of the Old World, but turbulent beginnings prevented this from happening. Old Saybrook, nevertheless, draws crowds to its fine beaches, yachting facilities, and shoreline cottages in Fenwick.

Bob's Bouillabaise

This recipe comes from the contributor's father. It serves a crowd and is traditionally served with French bread for dipping into the broth. Although not a "cheap eat", it is well worth the time and cost.

¼   cup olive oil
2   cups chopped onion
2   cups chopped leeks, white part only
½   cup chopped celery
1   (8-ounce) can tomato paste
½   teaspoon dried thyme
1   tablespoon minced garlic
3   ripe tomatoes, peeled, seeded and chopped
1   cup dry red wine
10   cups fish stock or bottled clam juice
     Tabasco sauce to taste
     raw meat from 2 lobsters
1   (3½ pound) striped bass, cut into 2 inch pieces
20   large shrimp, shelled and deveined
20   mussels, scrubbed
20   Littleneck clams
2   tablespoons Pernod
     salt and pepper to taste (see note)

1.   Heat the oil in a large skillet or Dutch oven and sauté the onions, leeks, and celery for about 5 minutes over medium-low heat until softened. Add tomato paste, thyme, garlic, chopped tomatoes, and wine. Bring to a boil, lower heat and simmer 30 minutes, stirring occasionally.
2.   Add fish stock, Tabasco sauce and bring to a boil. Add lobster, bass, shrimp, mussels, and clams. Reduce heat and simmer until fish is cooked and mussels and clams are opened, 5-8 minutes.

3. Stir in Pernod and season with salt and pepper. Serve immediately.

NOTE: If you are using bottled clam juice, you will probably not need any additional salt.

PREPARATION TIME: 2½-3 hours
YIELD: 10 servings

Crab and Corn Chowder

Adapted from a recipe from the Junior League of York, Pennsylvania.

2   cups frozen white corn
½   cup finely diced carrots
½   cup finely diced celery
¼   cup diced scallions
1   (10½ ounce) can chicken broth
2½   cups King Crab claw meat
1¼   teaspoon "Old Bay" seasoning
1½   cup (approximately) half and half or light cream
     salt and pepper to taste
     chopped parsley and paprika for garnish

1. Simmer the vegetables in the broth for 8-10 minutes or until just tender. Add the crabmeat and seasoning. Simmer about 5 minutes. Add enough cream to cover the ingredients in the pan. Season with salt and pepper and heat, but do not boil.
2. Serve sprinkled with a little parsley and paprika.

PREPARATION TIME: 20 minutes
YIELD: 4 servings

My Clam and Fish Chowder

4 dozen cherrystone clams
1 cup water
1 stick (8 tablespoons) butter
1 very large onion, chopped fine
1 cup dry white wine
8 medium-sized potatoes, peeled and cubed
1½ pounds or more mild white fish such as scrod or pollack, bones removed—a single thick fillet is preferred
¾ teaspoon ground thyme
    generous ¼ teaspoon cayenne pepper
3-4 pints (6-8 cups) half and half cream
    salt, as desired

1. Scrub clams under running water to remove all traces of sand.
2. In a large kettle, bring one cup of water to boil. Add about a dozen clams to the pot and cover. Steam over high heat just until they open. As clams open, remove from pot to a large bowl. Repeat the process in batches with remaining clams, discarding those which fail to open. Remove clams from shells and set aside, preserving all the broth. Collect broth from shells and pot together and pour through a strainer lined with 2 thicknesses of paper towels to remove any sand or grit. Set aside. You should have 4-5 cups.
3. In a large kettle, melt the butter and sauté onion over medium heat until soft and golden. Add strained broth and the wine and bring to the boil. Reduce over high heat for 5 minutes to concentrate broth.
4. Meanwhile, peel and dice potatoes. Add to the pot and return to the boil. Lower heat, cover, and simmer for 15 minutes or until potatoes are tender but firm.
5. Place fish on top of potatoes and simmer gently, breaking fish up with a wooden spoon, until fish tests done, about 5 minutes.

Do not boil chowder from this point on!

6. Add thyme and cayenne. Cut clams into small pieces and add to pot. Add the 3 or 4 pints of half and half, depending on how much soup is desired and on the flavor of the broth. Cook over low heat until just heated through, correct seasonings, and serve. Best if made a day ahead. Reheat very gently.

PREPARATION AND COOKING TIME: 1½ hours
YIELD: A huge pot—about 8-10 servings

Jackie's Corn and Clam Chowder

An easy and delicious family meal.

2   medium onions, chopped
2   tablespoons butter
1½   cups chicken broth
2   cups diced potatoes
1   bay leaf
¼   teaspoon celery salt
2   (7-ounce) cans minced clams
1   (16-ounce) can creamed corn
1   cup milk
1   cup half and half cream
      salt and pepper to taste

1. Sauté onions in butter for 3-5 minutes until softened. Add broth, potatoes, bay leaf, clams and celery salt. Cook about 20 minutes until potatoes are tender.
2. Add corn, milk, half and half and salt and pepper to taste. Heat thoroughly, but do not allow to boil.

PREPARATION TIME: 35 minutes
YIELD: 6 servings

Aunt Phyllis's Clam Fritters

Clam fritters are a New England specialty especially popular in shorefront eateries. Great served as an accompaniment to chowder or as a snack.

1   *egg*
3   *tablespoons vegetable oil*
¾   *cup clam juice*
¼   *cup milk*
1½ *cups flour*
2   *teaspoons baking powder*
¼   *teaspoon salt*
1   *cup chopped clams*
     oil for frying

1. Beat egg and oil together and add clam juice and milk.
2. Sift together flour, baking powder and salt. Add to egg mixture along with the chopped clams and stir to thoroughly combine.
3. In a large deep frying pan or a deep fryer heat oil to 370 degrees or until a drop of water sizzles when it hits the surface. Dip a teaspoon in oil before spooning out 1-1½ teaspoons of batter for each fritter. Drop batter into hot fat, making only 8 or so at one time so you do not crowd the pan. Fry fritters until they are puffed and golden brown, turning once with tongs, about 3 minutes. Remove with tongs or a slotted spoon and drain on paper towels.

PREPARATION AND COOKING TIME: 40 minutes
YIELD: approximately 2 dozen

Old Saybrook was the original home of Yale University in 1701. Yale moved to its present New Haven location fifteen years later.

Clinton Crab Bisque

To enhance the flavor of the bisque remove pot from the heat and let it sit for about 20 minutes. Return to a low burner and reheat gently before serving.

1	*pound fresh crabmeat*
6	*tablespoons unsalted butter*
1	*tablespoon flour*
4	*cups light cream*
½	*teaspoon Worcestershire sauce*
¼	*teaspoon ground mace*
1	*teaspoon salt*
¼	*teaspoon ground white pepper*
5	*tablespoons Sherry*
½	*cup whipping cream, whipped to soft peaks*
	paprika for garnish

1. Pick through the crab, removing any pieces of shell and cartilage. Set aside.
2. In a large heavy saucepan melt the butter, stir in the flour, and cook, stirring, over medium heat for 1 minute. Gradually stir in the light cream and add the Worcestershire and mace and the crabmeat. Simmer over low heat, stirring occasionally, for 20 minutes. Season with salt, white pepper, and Sherry.
3. Serve in soup bowls and top each serving with a dollop of whipped cream and a sprinkling of paprika.

PREPARATION AND COOKING TIME: 35 minutes
YIELD: 6 servings

During his teen years, playwright Eugene O'Neill was regularly thrown off the beach in Waterford. Today, the Eugene O'Neill Theater Center adjoins this very beach.

East Coast Cioppino

This recipe originated with the contributor's father. Serve it at an informal gathering and provide bibs and finger bowls!

¼   cup olive oil
2   tablespoons butter
2   medium onions, chopped
4   cloves garlic, minced
½   cup chopped green pepper
1   pound mushrooms, cut in half or sliced if large
1   one-pound can Italian plum tomatoes
1   6-ounce can tomato paste
2   cups dry red wine
½   cup fresh lemon juice
2   teaspoons dried basil
½   teaspoon dried oregano
1½   pounds red snapper, cut in bite-sized pieces
½   pound sea scallops
24   medium shrimp, shelled and deveined
12   cherrystone clams, shells scrubbed
1   pound Alaskan King or Snow Crab legs, broken into pieces
     (optional)
     salt and pepper to taste

1. In a large soup pot heat the oil and butter and sauté the onions and garlic over medium heat for 4 minutes. Add green pepper and mushrooms and cook for another 4 minutes. Add tomatoes, tomato paste, wine, lemon juice, basil and oregano, bring to the boil, reduce heat, and simmer, covered, for one hour. May be prepared ahead up to this point.
2. If base is made ahead, return to the simmer. Add the snapper, scallops, shrimp, clams and optional crab legs. Cook over low heat for 5-10 minutes or until clam shells open. Taste and season with salt and pepper if desired. Serve in shallow soup plates.

PREPARATION AND COOKING TIME: 1½ hours
YIELD: 6-8 servings

★Crab and Spinach Chowder

This is a family recipe and can be varied by substituting lobster or shrimp for the crab.

6-8 *ounces fresh, frozen, or canned crabmeat*
1   *(10-ounce) package fresh or frozen spinach*
3   *tablespoons butter*
½   *cup chopped onion*
2   *tablespoons flour*
½   *teaspoon salt*
      pinch white pepper
2   *cups chicken broth*
2   *cups half and half cream*
¾   *cup shredded cheddar cheese*

1. Pick over the crabmeat for cartilage and small bones. Cut the crabmeat into bite-sized pieces. Reserve any liquid from the crab.
2. Cook spinach slightly, drain and coarsely chop.
3. Melt butter in a large saucepan. Add onion and sauté 3-5 minutes until tender. Blend in flour and seasonings. Cook, stirring, about 2 minutes over medium-low heat. Gradually add the chicken broth, stirring constantly. Heat to boiling, stirring over medium heat. Cook 2 minutes.
4. Add half and half and any reserved crab liquid. Reduce heat to low and add crab, spinach and cheese. Cook just until heated through. Do not allow to boil.

NOTE: If using fresh spinach, wash and remove stems. Cook 2 minutes on high in the microwave.

PREPARATION TIME: 20 minutes
YIELD: 4-6 servings

★Wendell's Fish Chowder

An original recipe! The flavor is even better if made a day ahead.

4	*medium potatoes*
1	*stalk celery*
1	*medium onion*
2	*chicken bouillon cubes*
½	*pound chowder fish such as cod, pollack, or scrod*
2	*tablespoons unsalted butter*
3	*tablespoons white flour*
1	*(12-ounce) can evaporated milk*
2	*cups whole or low-fat milk*
1	*tablespoon lemon juice*
3-4	*tablespoons minced parsley*
	salt and pepper to taste

1. Wash potatoes and celery. (Leave skins on potatoes for best nutritional value.) Cube potatoes. Chop celery and onion.
2. Place vegetables and bouillon cubes in a large saucepan. Boil in water to cover for 8-10 minutes until potatoes are tender, but not mushy. Turn the heat down to medium-low and add the whole fish fillet. Cook about 8-10 minutes until fish is just cooked through.
3. Meanwhile, in a small saucepan, melt the butter over medium heat. Add the flour, stirring constantly with a whisk. Continue to stir and add the evaporated milk, ¼ cup at a time. Stir the sauce over medium heat until thick, creamy and bubbly. Remove from heat.
4. Pour the 2 cups of milk into the fish and vegetables and turn the heat down to low. Add the cream sauce and stir to blend all ingredients. Add the lemon juice, parsley and salt and pepper to taste.

PREPARATION TIME: 30 minutes
YIELD: 4 servings

Spicy Fish Soup

This is a hearty winter meal served with rice and Kim Chi.

1½ *pounds red snapper fillets, cut into serving pieces*
4   *cups water*
1   *pear, peeled, cored and sliced thinly*
4   *scallions, cut into 2 inch lengths*
4   *fresh shittake mushrooms, sliced*
1   *teaspoon fresh grated gingerroot*
2   *cloves garlic, minced*
2   *tablespoons soy sauce*
1   *tablespoon chili paste (available in some supermarkets and in Oriental markets)*
1   *teaspoon salt or to taste*
2   *teaspoons sugar*
    fresh ground pepper to taste
    White rice
    Kim Chi (pickled cabbage, available in Oriental markets)

1. Place all ingredients in a soup pot. Bring to a boil, reduce heat and simmer covered for about 10 minutes until fish flakes easily with a fork.
2. Serve with rice and Kim Chi.

PREPARATION TIME: 30 minutes
YIELD: 4 servings

In New England there sometimes appears a terrible pink mixture with tomatoes in it called Manhattan clam chowder and should not be confused with New England clam chowder, nor spoken of in the same breath. The old time New England Yankee says that tomatoes and clams have no more affinity than ice cream and horseradish!

★Connecticut Coastline Seafood Chowder

You can't beat the powerful aroma of this chowder simmering on the stove on a chilly afternoon.

Chowder Base

¼	*pound diced salt pork*
2	*large onions, peeled and chopped*
2	*leeks, cleaned and sliced*
1	*rib celery, sliced*
1	*cup water*
2	*cups Doxie clam juice or fish stock*
3	*cups peeled and diced potatoes*
1	*tablespoon chopped parsley*
½	*teaspoon oregano*
½	*teaspoon thyme*
1	*bay leaf, broken in half*
	freshly ground pepper

Ingredients to Finish Chowder

½	*pound bay scallops*
½	*pound firm white fish, cubed*
3	*dozen Quohogs (or any kind of clams), coarsely chopped*
4	*cups light cream*
	few drops Tabasco
2	*tablespoons unsalted butter*

1. Cook the salt pork in a large soup kettle over medium heat until fat is rendered and pork is crisp. Add onions and leeks and sauté for 4 minutes. Add remaining chowder base ingredients to the pot, bring to the boil, reduce heat and simmer, covered, for about 15 minutes or until potatoes are tender. Cool base and chill overnight if possible.

2. Return pot to stove and bring base to a simmer. Add seafood, including any clam liquor, and simmer for 3 minutes. Add remaining ingredients and cook over low heat until just heated through. Serve chowder immediately.

PREPARATION AND COOKING TIME: 1 hour
YIELD: 8 servings

Haddock Chowder

Serve with oyster crackers or saltines. The chowder improves if allowed to sit for a day before serving, but is also perfectly delicious if eaten immediately.

2   *tablespoons butter*
1   *large onion, chopped*
4   *cups sliced potatoes*
1   *12-ounce can niblet corn*
1   *pound haddock*
2   *13-ounce cans evaporated milk*
    salt and black pepper to taste

1. Melt the butter in a large saucepan and cook the onions over low heat until soft. Add potatoes and enough water to cover. Cover pot and simmer for 15-20 minutes until potatoes are tender.
2. Add corn to pot, place fish on top of the corn, cover and simmer over low heat until fish turns white, about 5 minutes. Gently stir in evaporated milk, breaking fish up into chunks but not stirring so hard that it completely shreds. Cook over low heat for 5 minutes. Season with salt and black pepper to taste.

PREPARATION AND COOKING TIME: 45 minutes
YIELD: 6 servings

Quebec Oyster Soup

Lawrence Lewis of Maine, the creater of this recipe, says, "C'est magni-
fique when preceded by two martinis each mixed six to one!"

½   *cup (8 tablespoons) butter*
3   *cups finely chopped celery*
3   *cups finely chopped green onions*
3   *cups finely chopped leeks*
1   *grated carrot*
1   *pint (2 cups) milk*
1   *pint (2 cups) light cream*
1   *teaspoon salt*
¼   *teaspoon pepper*
½   *teaspoon summer savory*
½   *cup white wine*
4   *cups (2 pounds) shucked oysters*

1.   Melt butter in a large sauce pan or soup pot. Add the celery,
     green onions, leeks and carrot and cook for 20 minutes over low
     heat, stirring occasionally. Add milk and cream and cook another
     20 minutes over low heat. Add salt, pepper and savory and sim-
     mer for 5 minutes.
2.   Meanwhile, bring the wine to a boil in a medium saucepan. Add
     the oysters, cover the pan and remove from the heat. Let stand
     for 20 minutes. Pour oysters and liquid into the soup pot. Serve hot.

NOTE: If thicker soup is desired, add ¼ cup of flour to the vegetables after they are cooked, then stir constantly as you add milk
and cream.

PREPARATION AND COOKING TIME: 1 hour
YIELD: 6 as an entree, 10 as a soup course

Christmas Eve Oyster Stew

A family tradition brought over from Ireland. The oysters need to be fresh and the sherry is a must!

½   cup (8 tablespoons) butter
2   teaspoons Worcestershire sauce
6   dashes Tabasco sauce
2   pints fresh shucked oysters, undrained
8   cups half and half or 4 cups whipping cream and 4 cups whole milk
    salt and white pepper to taste
½   cup dry sherry
    butter
    paprika
    oyster crackers, optional

1. In a 4-quart soup pot, slowly heat butter until melted. Add Worcestershire and Tabasco sauce. Over moderate heat, add the oysters and liquid. Simmer until edges of oysters curl, 3-4 minutes.
2. Add half and half and heat until warmed through, but not boiling. Add sherry and salt and pepper to taste.
3. Serve in individual bowls dotted with butter and sprinkled with paprika. Serve oyster crackers alongside if desired.

NOTE: Soup should be eaten soon after preparation, but it can be held at room temperature for about an hour. Reheat gently, without allowing to boil, just before serving.

PREPARATION TIME: 30 minutes
YIELD: 8-10 small rich servings

Seafood Stew Manhattan-Style

It's the tomatoes that give this a Manhattan aura.

3   *tablespoons butter*
1   *medium onion*
2   *ribs celery*
1   *clove garlic*
1   *(one pound) can crushed plum tomatoes in puree or one can*
       plum tomatoes
2   *cups chicken stock or 1 cup bottled clam juice plus 1 cup water*
1   *teaspoon dried thyme*
1   *bay leaf, broken in half*
¼   *teaspoon dried red pepper flakes*
1   *pound firm, non-oily fish such as cod, haddock, halibut or*
       monkfish
12-16 *mussels*
½   *cup chopped Italian parsley*
1   *tablespoon chopped fresh tarragon or 1 teaspoon dried*
       salt to taste
       black pepper to taste

1. Melt the butter in a heavy 4-quart pot. Chop the onion and the celery and mince the garlic. Cook the vegetables in the butter over medium heat until softened, about 3 minutes. Add the tomatoes and the chicken stock or clam juice and water. Add thyme, bay leaf and pepper flakes. Bring to a boil and simmer partially covered for 10 minutes.
2. Cut the fish into 1½-inch cubes. Scrub the mussels and pull off their beards.
3. Stir parsley and tarragon into the stew and add the fish, stirring in gently. Arrange the mussels on the top. Cover and cook on

low heat until mussels have steamed open and the fish is opaque, about 5 minutes. Discard the bay leaf and season with salt and pepper. Serve in shallow bowls with toasted French bread.

PREPARATION AND COOKING TIME: 35 minutes
YIELD: 4 servings

Mussel Soup with Saffron Cream

Serve with toasted buttered pita breads sprinkled with Parmesan cheese.

3	*tablespoons butter*
3	*tablespoons coarsely chopped shallots or scallions*
3	*tablespoons coarsely chopped onion*
½	*clove garlic, minced*
½	*teaspoon saffron threads*
1½	*quarts mussels, scrubbed and debearded*
1	*cup dry white wine*
¼	*cup chopped parsley*
	few drops of Tabasco
2	*cups heavy cream*

1. Melt butter in a large kettle and sauté shallots, onion, garlic and saffron for 3 minutes. Add mussels, wine, parsley and Tabasco and bring to a boil. Cover pot, lower heat and simmer until mussels open, about 5 minutes.
2. Remove mussels with a slotted spoon and add cream to the pot. Simmer uncovered until liquid is reduced by about one-fourth. Return mussels to pot to heat through. Ladle soup into shallow bowls and serve.

PREPARATION AND COOKING TIME: 30 minutes
YIELD: 4 servings

New Haven and Bridgeport

As the home of Yale University, New Haven, at first called Quinnipiac, and changed later for the English seaport in Sussex, England, is one of New England's most popular cities. When New Haven was planned back in 1683, it was conceived as a model village laid out in little squares bound by narrow streets. It may, in fact, be the first example of city planning in America. The town green of today was once a marketplace and pastureland, while the parcel of land on which Yale stands was set aside as "college land".

In days gone by, oyster farming was present along the waterfront which was also homeport for a good sized fleet of cargo carriers. Today, the waterfront is the third largest seaport in New England. The *MV Liberty Bell* has replaced the schooners and square riggers of yesteryear; sailing from May to October, she takes passengers on sightseeing tours along the New Haven coastline. Lighthouse Point Park, a popular recreational spot, is situated at the point where the waters of the harbor meet Long Island Sound.

Just east of New Haven are the picturesque towns of Madison, Guilford and Branford, often referred to as the "Shoreline" communities. At the turn of the century they were popular as summer resorts for the wealthy; the elegant seaside homes which remain, are reflective of that era. Once referred to as the "Newport" of Connecticut, their town greens still are among the most beautiful in New England. Offshore from Branford are the scenic Thimble Islands which are dotted with stately homes. These islands are also a favorite spot of the yachting community.

Farther along the coastline is the city of Bridgeport, where the shipbuilding trade of the 1700's along the banks of the Pequonnock River launched the town's reputation as a seaport. Black Rock Harbor was a well known shipping point, and ships that sailed from her port carried passengers, freight and mail as they sailed as far away as the West Indies. In the late 1890's, select oysters from her waterfront beds were transported from coast to coast as well as to ports of Europe.

Whale fishing claimed no small amount of attention. The horizon was often the sight of whaling vessels sailing into Bridgeport harbor with great crowds assembling at the water's edge to welcome

PASTAS

the mariners home from their long voyages from as far away as the South Atlantic and Indian Oceans. One such voyage of the *Atlantic* lasted 629 days and netted a capture of thirty-four whales.

The waterfront of today is still a boom of activity serving as a gateway to Long Island by way of regular ferry transportation. Its Seaside Park, designed by Fredrick Law Olmsted of Central Park fame, encompasses two and one-half miles along Long Island Sound. The stretch of beach is not only a playground for sunbathers but is a paradise for strollers, cyclists and joggers.

In the Black Rock section of the city is a quaint maritime village known as Captain's Cove Seaport which features the *H.M.S. Rose*, an authentic replica of a British warship. This area, with its 400-boat marina and charming shops, serves as a reminder that the waterfront will once again bring Bridgeport back to its "days of glory".

Linguine with Clams and Mushrooms

Angel hair pasta is also great with this sauce.

1   *pound mushrooms*
½   *cup (8 tablespoons) butter*
3   *cloves garlic, minced*
1   *pound minced fresh clams (about 3 cups), undrained*
½   *cup chopped parsley*
1   *teaspoon salt, or to taste*
¼   *teaspoon ground black pepper*
1   *pound linguine, fresh or dried, cooked according to package*
     directions

1. Clean the mushrooms, slice them and set aside. Melt the butter
    in a large skillet and sauté the garlic over medium heat for one
    minute. Add the mushrooms and sauté for about 5 minutes,
    stirring frequently. Add clams, including any liquid, along with
    the parsley, salt and pepper. Mix well and simmer for a few
    minutes, uncovered, to blend flavors.
2. Serve over cooked linguine.

PREPARATION AND COOKING TIME: 30 minutes
YIELD: 6 servings

Barb's Linguine with Clams

1   *pound linguine*
⅓   *cup olive oil*
5   *cloves garlic, minced*
1   *dozen fresh clams, chopped (including any juice)*
1   *8-ounce bottle clam juice*
¼   *cup white wine*
2   *tablespoons chopped parsley*
     dash of red pepper flakes

1. Cook linguine according to package directions.
2. Heat oil in a large skillet and sauté garlic over low heat until lightly browned. Add clams and clam juice, wine, parsley and pepper flakes. Simmer uncovered for 5 minutes.
3. Drain pasta. Add a small amount of the sauce to the pasta and toss. Pour pasta into a serving dish and pour remaining sauce over the top.

PREPARATION AND COOKING TIME: 20 minutes
YIELD: 4 servings

Tagliarini with Smoked Salmon

Leba and Neil Sedaka donated this recipe.

1   *pound tagliarini, preferably fresh*
4   *tablespoons olive oil*
2   *shallots, minced*
4   *ounces smoked salmon, cut in julienne strips*
7   *ounces plum tomatoes, peeled, seeded and chopped*
½   *cup heavy cream*
1   *pinch nutmeg*
    salt to taste

1. Cook tagliarini in a large pot of boiling salted water until it is al dente. Drain.
2. While pasta is cooking, heat olive oil in a 4-quart saucepan over low heat. Add shallots and sauté until translucent. Add all other ingredients and simmer gently for 2 minutes. Add drained pasta and toss over low heat until well-coated with sauce and heated through.

NOTE: If tagliarini is unavailable, use any very thin-strand pasta.

PREPARATION AND COOKING TIME: 20 minutes
YIELD: 4 first course servings

Steamed Mussels on Pasta

Our contributor is not sure
where she got this recipe but
she thinks it might have been
off a bag of mussels! She loves to serve mussels because not only are they
high in protein and low in calories, they're also inexpensive.

2   *pounds mussels*
2   *tablespoons olive oil, margarine or butter*
¼   *cup chopped onion*
2   *cloves garlic, finely chopped*
1   *cup dry wine or beer or low-salt chicken broth*
     freshly chopped parsley
12   *ounces linguine, cooked according to package directions and*
     drained

1.   Remove the "beards" from the mussels by pulling toward the
     small end of the mussel. Rinse mussels well in cold water.
2.   In a large saucepan over medium heat, sauté the onion and garlic
     in the oil for 1 minute. Add mussels and wine, cover, and cook
     over medium-high heat for about 5 minutes, occasionally stir-
     ring pot so mussels cook evenly. Shells will open when mussels
     are done.
3.   Place cooked linguine on a large platter, pour mussels and juice
     over pasta, sprinkle with chopped parsley and serve. Offer lots
     of crusty bread for dipping up the sauce.

PREPARATION AND COOKING TIME: 25 minutes
YIELD: 4 servings

*In 1835 in Bridgeport, Phineas T. Barnum founded the circus which
eventually became known as the "Greatest Show On Earth". Barnum was
also a former mayor of the city.*

★Fresh Vermicelli with Smoked Salmon and Cream

From Chef John Braun of Le Coq Hardi restaurants in Ridgefield and Stamford, CT.

1	tablespoon sweet butter
4	tablespoons capers
2	leeks, white part only, rinsed and cut into julienne
3	cups fish stock, white wine, or white stock
1	cup heavy cream
3	sticks (24 tablespoons) sweet butter, softened
20	thin slices of carrot, blanched briefly
20	sugar snaps or snow peas, blanched briefly
2	tomatoes, peeled, seeded and cut into julienne
12	ounces vermicelli (preferably fresh), cooked and drained
8	ounces smoked Norwegian salmon, cut paper thin at a bias angle
4	teaspoons chopped fresh chervil or parsley

1. Melt the tablespoon of butter in a skillet and sauté the capers and julienned leeks gently until soft but not colored. Add the fish stock and reduce over medium heat by three-fourths to about ¾ cup. Add cream and reduce sauce base to about ½ cup. Remove pan from heat and stir in the softened butter, a couple of table-spoons at a time, to form a smooth, creamy sauce. Return pan to low heat momentarily if necessary to incorporate butter.

2. Heat pasta by plunging briefly into a pot of boiling water. Drain and place in warm serving bowl or on a platter. Add carrots, snow peas and tomatoes to sauce to heat through. Pour sauce over pasta and arrange slices of smoked salmon over the top. Sprinkle with chopped herbs and serve.

PREPARATION AND COOKING TIME: 45 minutes
YIELD: 4 main course servings
8 first course servings

Captain's Cove Shrimp and Pasta

½   pound medium shrimp, peeled and deveined
⅔   pound pasta, preferably fresh
1   tomato, diced
1   scallion, chopped fine
½   cup light cream or half and half, plus additional if necessary
2   tablespoons butter or margarine
1   ounce grated Parmesan cheese
    salt and pepper to taste
    pinch of thyme or parsley if desired

1. Cut the shrimp in half and set aside.
2. Cook the pasta in a large pot of boiling salted water. Fresh pasta takes about 3 minutes, dried about 8 minutes. Add shrimp to pasta and water for final 60 seconds of cooking. Drain pasta and shrimp into a colander and return to the cooking pot.
3. Add tomatoes, scallions, cream, butter, and Parmesan cheese and toss over a warm burner for one minute until creamy. Add a little more cream if necessary to make enough sauce to coat pasta. Add salt and pepper and optional herb to taste. Serve on warm plates.

PREPARATION AND COOKING TIME: 20 minutes
YIELD: 4 servings

Scallop or Shrimp Marinara

⅓   cup olive oil
2   cloves garlic, minced
4   cups tomatoes, peeled and chopped
1   tablespoon chopped parsley
½   teaspoon dried basil or 1 tablespoon fresh
½   teaspoon salt
¼   teaspoon fresh ground pepper
⅛   teaspoon dried oregano or 1½ teaspoons fresh
3   tablespoons tomato paste
1   pound sea scallops or 1 pound large shrimp, shelled and deveined
1   pound thin spaghetti, cooked al dente

1. Heat oil in a large saucepan and cook garlic over low heat until very lightly browned. Add tomatoes, parsley, basil, salt and pepper and simmer slowly for 30 minutes, stirring often. Add oregano and tomato paste and continue to cook about 15 minutes or until sauce is quite thick.
2. Add either the scallops or the shrimp and simmer until shellfish is slightly firm to the touch, but not overcooked, about 4 minutes.
3. Serve over hot pasta.

PREPARATION AND COOKING TIME: 1 hour
YIELD: 4 servings

★Shoreline Seafood Fettuccine

8	ounces fettuccine noodles
2	tablespoons butter for cooking seafood
½	pound medium shrimp, shelled and deveined
1	6-ounce package frozen crabmeat, thawed
1	teaspoon dried basil
4	tablespoons butter, melted
½	cup grated Parmesan
½	cup whipping cream, plus additional if needed
	salt and freshly ground pepper to taste
	chopped parsley for garnish

1. Cook the fettuccine in a large pot of boiling salted water according to package directions.
2. In a large skillet, melt the 2 tablespoons butter, add the shrimp and crab and sauté over medium heat until the shrimp turns pink, approximately 3 minutes. Sprinkle with the basil.
3. When pasta is done, drain thoroughly and toss with the melted butter, Parmesan, and about ½ cup of cream, or enough to coat the noodles well. Pour seafood mixture over fettuccine and toss to combine. Season with salt and freshly ground pepper to taste and sprinkle with chopped parsley before serving.

PREPARATION AND COOKING TIME: 30 minutes
YIELD: 4 servings

Linguine with Squid

Adapted from a recipe in a 1986 issue of COOK'S Magazine.

1½ *pounds cleaned squid*
4   *cloves garlic, unpeeled*
1   *pound linguine, preferably the imported kind such as DeCecco*
3   *tablespoons olive oil*
1   *teaspoon red pepper flakes*
½-1 *teaspoon salt (optional)*
½   *cup heavy cream*
4   *tablespoons chopped parsley*
2   *scallions, minced*
5-6 *oil packed sun-dried tomatoes, chopped*
4   *tablespoons shredded fresh basil or 1 teaspoon dried*

1. Cut squid into slices the same width as the linguine. Keep tentacles whole or cut in half if very large. Set aside.
2. Bring a large pot of water to the boil. Add the unpeeled garlic and blanch for 5 minutes. Remove with a slotted spoon. Slip the skin off the garlic, mince, and set aside.
3. Add 1 tablespoon salt to the water and cook the pasta at a rapid boil until cooked al dente. Drain and rinse.
4. Heat the olive oil in a very large skillet until very hot. Add the squid pieces and the red pepper flakes and the optional salt. Cook, stirring continuously, until the squid all turns opaque, no more than 2 minutes. Add the cream, parsley, scallions, sundried tomatoes, minced garlic and the cooked linguine. Toss over medium heat until heated through. Add basil and toss again. Taste and correct seasoning if necessary.

PREPARATION AND COOKING TIME: 35 minutes
YIELD: 4 large main course servings
          8 first course servings

Seafood Noodle Casserole

Make in the morning and heat for dinner.

3   *cups uncooked noodles*
3   *tablespoons butter for noodles*
½   *pound fresh mushrooms*
2   *tablespoons butter*
1   *cup light cream*
1   *10-ounce can cream of mushroom soup*
¾   *cup grated sharp cheddar cheese*
1   *pound cooked shrimp*
2   *cups cooked crabmeat*
1   *cup soft fresh bread crumbs*
1   *tablespoon melted butter*

1. Cook noodles in a large pot of boiling water according to package directions. Drain and toss with the 3 tablespoons butter.
2. Slice the mushrooms. In a large skillet heat the 2 tablespoons butter and sauté mushrooms over medium heat for about 5 minutes, shaking the pan frequently.
3. Combine cream, undiluted soup and cheese and pour over noodles. Add mushrooms, shrimp and crabmeat and toss gently to combine. Transfer to a buttered 3-quart casserole, top with crumbs and drizzle with the tablespoon melted butter. Casserole may be made ahead to this point, covered, and refrigerated.
4. Preheat oven to 350 degrees. Bake casserole uncovered for about 30 minutes or until lightly browned on top and bubbly around the edges.

PREPARATION TIME: 30 minutes
COOKING TIME: 30 minutes
YIELD: 6 servings.

Shrimp and Crab Madeira
on Linguine

4   tablespoons butter
2   tablespoons minced shallots
1   cup sliced mushrooms
¾   pound shrimp, peeled and deveined
8   ounces crabmeat
½   cup Madeira
¼   teaspoon dried tarragon
1   tablespoon lemon juice
2   teaspoons tomato paste
2   egg yolks
1   cup heavy cream
      salt and pepper to taste
12   ounces linguine, cooked al dente and drained
2   tablespoons minced parsley for garnish

1. In a large non-reactive skillet, melt the butter and sauté the
    shallots over low heat until soft. Raise the heat, add the mush-
    rooms and sauté until lightly browned and liquid has evapo-
    rated, about 5 minutes. Add shrimp and cook, stirring, for one
    minute. Add crab breaking it up gently so that most of lumps
    remain. Pour Madeira into pan and simmer until almost com-
    pletely evaporated. Add tarragon, lemon juice and tomato paste
    and mix gently to combine.
2. In a small bowl, combine egg yolks with cream. Remove skillet
    from heat, slowly stir in egg/cream mixture, return to low heat
    and cook, stirring constantly, just until sauce is heated through.
    Do not allow to boil or sauce will curdle. Season with salt and
    pepper to taste.
3. Serve over linguine and sprinkle parsley over the top.

PREPARATION AND COOKING TIME: 30 minutes
YIELD: 4 servings

Seafood Vermicelli

The choice of seafood can be varied here depending on what is available in the market.

3	tablespoons olive oil
1	large onion, chopped
1	large green pepper, seeded and diced
2	cloves garlic, minced
1	1-pound can crushed tomatoes
1	8-ounce can tomato sauce
¾	of a small can (6-ounce) tomato paste
¾	cup white wine
¼	cup vermouth
½	cup chopped parsley
1	teaspoon oregano
1	teaspoon salt
⅛	teaspoon pepper
½	pound shrimp, peeled and deveined
½	pound sea scallops
½	pound monkfish or halibut, cut in 1½-inch chunks
1	dozen littleneck clams, scrubbed
1	pound vermicelli, cooked and drained

1. Heat oil in a large saucepan. Add onions, green pepper and garlic and cook over medium heat for 2-3 minutes. Add crushed tomatoes, tomato sauce and tomato paste, wine, vermouth, parsley, oregano, salt and pepper. Bring to the boil, lower heat and simmer covered for 30 minutes.
2. Add prepared seafood and cook about 10 minutes, until clam shells open.
3. Serve over hot vermicelli.

PREPARATION AND COOKING TIME: 45 minutes
YIELD: 6 servings

The Maritime Center at Norwalk

The Maritime Center at Norwalk is a unique waterfront museum complex which focuses on the marine environment and maritime heritage of Long Island Sound. Located in the revitalized historic district of South Norwalk, or SoNo, it offers the visitor the opportunity to explore man's past, present and future relationship with the sea. Nineteenth century industrial architecture has been combined with new buildings to house the Maritime Center which overlooks the Norwalk River.

The three major components of the Center are the Marine World, the Maritime Exhibits, and an IMAX theater. Each attraction allows the visitor to actively participate in a learning experience. One can view the sea as it is seen by the scientist, the diver, the marine historian, the fisherman, and the sailor.

In the Marine World the visitor can "journey" from a Connecticut salt marsh to Long Island Sound and the Atlantic Ocean. The scale ranges from microscopic marine specimens to large fish and mammals. It is a continually changing experience in scale, light, mood, color,—all manipulated to provide an experience as various as the marine world itself.

The Center's History component focuses on the commercial and industrial life of Connecticut's thriving coastal communities in the nineteenth century. History comes alive as visitors view the crafts and commerce of the past all linked to the present. Current methods of wooden boatbuilding are demonstrated on an interactive basis.

The IMAX theater brings certain marine experiences to vivid life—experiences like sailing a square rigger around Cape Horn, or probing the ocean floor in a research submarine. The viewer is immersed in the sight and sound, and becomes a part of the visual experience.

SAUCES

The Junior League of Stamford-Norwalk is proud to have served as a founding member of the Maritime Center. The League has contributed financial support as well as hundreds of hours of volunteer manpower during the planning and development stages of the Center. It sponsors the "Sea Star" which is a hands-wet exhibit supervised by a League docent where individuals can handle live marine specimens and observe them at close range. A unique and exciting experience awaits you at the Maritime Center at Norwalk!

Zippy Cocktail Sauce

This recipe comes from a contributor's uncle in West Virginia. It's a great dipping sauce for cold shrimp, oysters or crab.

½   cup catsup
1   heaping tablespoon prepared horseradish (preferably Silver brand)
3   tablespoons sugar
1   tablespoon A-1 sauce
1½   teaspoons lemon juice
½   teaspoon Worcestershire sauce
8   drops Tabasco
     salt and freshly ground pepper to taste

1.   Combine all ingredients in a small bowl and mix well. Cover and refrigerate. Best if made a few hours ahead, and will keep several days in the refrigerator.

PREPARATION TIME: 5 minutes   YIELD: ¾ cup

Basil Dipping Sauce

1   cup loosely packed basil leaves
¼   cup soy sauce
1½   cups ketchup
1   teaspoon Worcestershire sauce
     a few drops Tabasco, or to taste
     whole fresh basil leaves for garnish

1.   Mince the basil leaves in a food processor or blender. Add remaining ingredients, except the garnish, and blend. Chill and taste again for seasoning. Serve in a small bowl garnished with basil leaves.

PREPARATION TIME: 10 minutes   YIELD: 2 cups

Watercress Sauce

An adaptation of a *Gourmet Magazine* recipe.

¾   *cup mayonnaise*
1   *tablespoon chili sauce*
1   *bunch watercress*
4   *sprigs parsley*
1   *teaspoon lemon juice*
½   *teaspoon Dijon mustard*
       salt and pepper to taste

1.   Place mayonnaise and chili sauce in the workbowl of a food pro-
      cessor or in a blender. Cut stems off watercress and parsley and
      add them, along with the lemon juice and mustard to the work-
      bowl. Process until smooth and blended. Season with salt and
      pepper to taste. Transfer to a small bowl and refrigerate for at
      least 1 hour before serving. May be made as much as one day
      ahead. Serve as a dip for cold shrimp or as a sauce for other
      seafood.

PREPARATION TIME: 10 minutes   YIELD: 1 cup

Steamer Sauce

A nice variation to the usual melted butter for steamers. This is a Fishers
Island favorite. The following recipe makes enough for 3 quarts of
steamers.

1   *stick (8 tablespoons) butter*
¼   *cup Worcestershire sauce*
½-1 *teaspoon garlic salt*

1.   Melt butter slowly in a saucepan. Add Worcestershire and garlic
      salt and stir to combine.

PREPARATION TIME: 5 minutes   YIELD: ¾ cup

Provençale Sauce for Fish

Just the kind of light, zesty accompaniment to nicely complement almost any variety of fish.

1   red ripe tomato, about 8 ounces
2   tablespoons red wine vinegar
¼   cup olive oil
¼   cup finely chopped shallots
1   teaspoon finely minced garlic
¼   cup finely chopped basil
½   teaspoon grated lemon zest
    salt and pepper to taste

1. Place tomato in boiling water for 10 seconds. Peel and core. Slice in half crosswise and gently squeeze out seeds. Chop into ¼-inch cubes. Toss in a bowl with remaining ingredients, seasoning to taste.

PREPARATION TIME: 20 minutes
YIELD: 1 cup

White Clam Sauce

½   cup olive oil
4   cloves garlic, minced
1   cup clam juice
½   cup water
1   quart shucked little necks and their liquor (or substitute 2 cups canned little necks)
1   tablespoon chopped parsley
    salt and pepper to taste

1. Heat oil in a large skillet and cook garlic over low heat until very lightly browned. Remove pan from heat and cool oil slightly. Pour in clam juice and water, very slowly at first to make sure it does not spatter. Add clams and simmer sauce uncovered for 5

minutes. Stir in parsley and season with salt and pepper to taste. Serve over cooked spaghetti or linguine.

NOTE: To open little necks, steam over boiling water until shells open. Remove clams and chop coarsely. Strain cooking liquid and use in sauce if desired.

PREPARATION AND COOKING TIME: 30 minutes
YIELD: 4-5 servings

Sauce Beurre Blanc

This sauce originates in France, and is delicious served with a fish terrine, mousse, or poached fish.

4   *large shallots*
⅓   *cup white wine vinegar*
⅓   *cup dry white wine*
2   *tablespoons crème frâiche*
1   *cup (16 tablespoons) butter*
    salt
    freshly ground white pepper

1. Chop the shallots very finely and combine them in a small, non-aluminum saucepan with the vinegar and wine. Simmer uncovered over medium heat until reduced to 1 tablespoon. Add the crème frâiche and simmer until slightly thickened.
2. Cut the butter into pieces. Add to the reduction in the saucepan over very low heat, whisking constantly. Butter should soften and thicken without turning oily. Season to taste with salt and pepper. Do not at any time let the sauce boil or it will separate. To keep warm, place on a rack over boiling water.

NOTE: If beurre blanc separates, add 1 tablespoon cold water to one side of saucepan and gradually whisk the separated sauce into the water.

PREPARATION AND COOKING TIME: 20 minutes
YIELD: 1¼ cups

Norwalk

Back in the days of glory when majestic schooners sailed into Norwalk's harbor and the oyster was king, Norwalk had a dependent link with the sea. The earliest settlers here were taught fishing and oystering techniques from the Indians as a means to survive. Local potteries produced "monkey jugs" or ceramic water coolers which were indispensable aboard whaling ships, along with oyster jars used in the shipment of Norwalk oysters. Schooners, such as the *Alice S. Wentworth* which was built in Norwalk in 1863, carried local products to distant ports. Cruise ships transported eager passengers to coastal destinations. In short, the waterfront was a hub of activity with sailors, sea merchants and passengers frequenting the local hotels, saloons, sail lofts and chandleries.

Oystering in the late 1800's was the chief fishing product of the United States and the most extensively eaten shellfish. At the peak of the industry, fifty large planters and shippers operated from Norwalk. The one remaining oyster company here today is said to be one of the largest in the world. Connecticut oysters are ranked by connoisseurs as among the finest, and they still fetch at least $10 more per bushel wholesale than their Chesapeake Bay counterparts!

Norwalk's rich relationship with the sea is being recaptured as the waterfront booms with activity once again. Riverfront historic buildings in the SoNo district have been revitalized into oyster and clam bars, restaurants, art galleries and charming shops recreating a bustling seaport town. Annually, the Oyster Festival, sponsored by the Norwalk Seaport Association, provides several days of fun and entertainment in celebration of the rich oyster harvest. The Seaport recently purchased the Sheffield Lighthouse, which has stood guard in Norwalk's harbor since 1868. Plans to preserve the character of the site and use it for multi-faceted educational programs are underway. Norwalk is home port for the "Little America's Cup" sailing race, the annual hot air balloon launching across the Sound,

ENTRÉES

SHEFFIELD (NORWALK)
LIGHTHOUSE

and boasts the largest in-water boat show on the east coast. The
Lady Joan, a replica of a paddle-wheel steamboat, takes passengers
on a cruise around the picturesque Norwalk Islands. The Maritime
Center focuses on the marine environment and maritime heritage
of Long Island Sound. Indeed, maritime history is still very much
alive in Norwalk today!

Striped Bass Fermiere

This is an old Nantucket recipe which a native gave to our contributor.
Don't ask how the French got into it!

4   *pounds skinless striped bass fillets*
12   *tablespoons butter, divided*
3   *carrots, scraped and cut into thin rounds*
1   *cup thinly sliced shallots*
1½   *cups thinly sliced celery*
4   *mushrooms, thinly sliced*
1½   *cups dry white wine*
     salt and pepper to taste
     juice of ½ lemon
1   *cup heavy cream*

1. Cut fish fillets slightly on the bias into 8 "steaks" and refrigerate.
2. Heat 6 tablespoons of the butter in a large stovetop casserole or
    non-reactive skillet. Add the carrots, shallots, celery and mush-
    rooms. Pour ⅓ cup of the wine over the vegetables and cook
    uncovered over medium-high heat until wine has been almost
    completely reduced, about 10 minutes. Add another ⅓ cup of
    wine and cook until that has been reduced, another 10 minutes.
3. Sprinkle fish pieces with salt and pepper and arrange them over
    the vegetables. Pour the remaining wine over the fish and bring
    to the boil. Lower heat, cover, and simmer for 6 minutes.
    Sprinkle lemon juice over fish, then carefully lift it out of the pot
    using a large spatula and transfer it to a serving platter and keep
    warm.
4. Add cream to liquid and vegetables remaining in the cooking pot,
    raise heat to high and cook, shaking the pan so that the cream
    blends with the vegetables, for 3 minutes.
5. Reduce heat to low. Cut remaining 6 tablespoons of butter into
    8 pieces and add it, one piece at a time while shaking and stir-
    ring to blend. Pour sauce over fish and serve.

PREPARATION AND COOKING TIME: 40 minutes **YIELD:** 8 servings

Bluefish Grilled in Foil

This recipe comes from Fishers Island and is a DuPont family favorite. The packet can be prepared ahead and stored for up to 12 hours before grilling.

2   *large bluefish fillets (about 1 pound each)*
1   *medium onion, thinly sliced*
1   *green pepper, seeded and thinly sliced*
1   *large firm tomato, thinly sliced*
1   *cup bottled Italian salad dressing*
    lemon wedges for garnish
    large pieces of aluminum foil

1. Prepare a barbecue fire. Coals should burn down until they are covered with a white ash.
2. Rinse and dry the bluefish. Tear off two pieces of aluminum foil large enough to wrap around the fish and seal it tightly.
3. On one sheet of foil, place one of the bluefish fillets, skin-side down. Layer sliced onion, green pepper and tomato on top. Top with the second fillet, skin-side up.
4. Raise the sides of the foil and pour the salad dressing over the fish. Seal foil by crimping the edges together and wrap again with the second sheet of foil.
5. Place the packet on the grill and cook for 20 minutes, turning once. Poke holes in foil with fork to let liquid escape and grill for another 5 minutes or so per side or until fish tests done.
6. Remove from grill, open foil and serve with lemon wedges.

PREPARATION TIME: 15 minutes
COOKING TIME: 20-30 minutes
YIELD: 4-6 servings

Fried Catfish Fillets

A wonderful Southern specialty!

⅔   cup self-rising cornmeal (see note)
½   cup self-rising flour (see note)
½   teaspoon salt
½   teaspoon freshly ground black pepper
1   egg
¼   cup milk
½   teaspoon prepared mustard
4   catfish fillets
     oil for frying
1   lemon, cut in wedges

1. In a small shallow bowl, combine the cornmeal, flour, salt, and
    pepper. In another small shallow bowl, combine the egg, milk,
    and mustard. Drop fillets first into the egg mixture and then coat
    with the cornmeal mixture. Chill fillets in a single layer on a plate
    for one minute in the refrigerator or while heating oil.
2. Heat about ½ inch oil to 350 degrees in a large frying pan. Fry
    fillets for about 6 minutes, turning once, until golden brown and
    the fish is cooked through.
3. Serve with lemon wedges.

NOTE: If self-rising cornmeal or flour is unavailable, add about ½
teaspoon baking powder to the flour mixture.

PREPARATION TIME: 15 minutes
COOKING TIME: 6 minutes
YIELD: 4 servings

*Starfish are the major predator of shellfish. Years ago fishermen would
tear them in two and throw them back into the sea, not realizing that the
starfish can regenerate lost arms and, thus, increase their population.*

Coastline Clambake

An adaptation of the traditional New England clambake.

Variable amounts of the following (see note below):
lobsters
steamer clams and/or mussels
seaweed (optional)
red potatoes, whole
small whole onions, peeled
corn on the cob, silk removed but some husk left on

1. Scrub clams and mussels. Layer all ingredients in the order listed in a large covered lobster pot or stock pot. Pour one quart of water over all. Bring to the boil and cook over medium heat for 45 minutes on the stove or one hour on a grill. Fork test potatoes for doneness.
2. Serve with plenty of melted butter for dipping.

PREPARATION AND COOKING TIME: 1-1½ hours
YIELD: Variable, depending on size of pot. Allow one lobster per person.

Tradition has it that each clambake has its own bakemaster. He supervises its preparation from the building of the fire to the placing of the clams, as well as the rest of the bake. His judgement fixes the time for opening the bake and to him goes the credit for its success. A good bakemaster is much sought after and is proud of his skill.

Maryland Crab Cakes

This recipe is an adaptation of one that appeared in *The New York Times* in about 1975.

1   *pound fresh lump crabmeat*
¼   *cup chopped parsley*
1   *cup minced scallions, including some green tops*
¾   *cup fresh bread crumbs*
2   *eggs*
¼   *cup milk*
4-5   *drops Tabasco*
1   *teaspoon Worcestershire sauce*
2   *tablespoons Dijon mustard*
   salt and black pepper to taste
   vegetable oil (preferably Wesson) for frying
1   *cup fresh bread crumbs for coating crab cakes*

1. Pick over crabmeat carefully and discard any shell bits. In a large bowl combine the crab with the parsley, scallions and bread crumbs. Mix well with a fork.
2. In a small bowl blend together the eggs, milk and seasonings. Pour over crab mixture and blend gently so as to leave crab lumps as whole as possible.
3. Pour enough oil into a large skillet to measure a depth of about ¾ inch. Heat oil over medium heat until hot but not smoking. Meanwhile shape the crab mixture into 6 cakes and dredge them lightly in the fresh bread crumbs to coat. Shallow fry the crab cakes until golden brown on both sides, 8-10 minutes total.
4. Preheat oven to 325 degrees. Place the cooked crab cakes on a baking sheet, cover loosely with foil and place in the oven for about 10 minutes to ensure that they are hot all the way through.

PREPARATION TIME: 20 minutes
COOKING TIME: 20 minutes
YIELD: 6 crab cakes

Sautéed Soft Shell Crabs

The simple and classic preparation adapted from a recipe from the American Seafood Institute is the best way to enjoy this East Coast seasonal delicacy!

12	*cleaned soft shell crabs*
1	*cup flour*
1	*teaspoon salt*
1	*teaspoon dried dillweed*
1	*teaspoon pepper*
½	*teaspoon baking powder*
½	*cup (8 tablespoons) butter*
2	*tablespoons oil*
½	*cup dry white wine*
2	*tablespoons butter for finishing the sauce*

1. Dry crabs with paper towels.
2. Mix flour, salt, dillweed, pepper, and baking powder in a large baggie. Shake each crab in the flour mixture and shake off excess.
3. Heat 4 tablespoons of the butter and 1 tablespoon of the oil in a large skillet and sauté as many crabs as will fit comfortably in the skillet until nicely browned, about 5 minutes per side. Sauté remaining crabs in the same manner, adding remaining 4 tablespoons butter and 1 tablespoon oil as necessary.
4. When crabs are cooked, add the wine to the skillet and cook, stirring up any browned bits clinging to the bottom, for about 2 minutes. Remove pan from the heat and stir in the 2 tablespoons butter. Pour sauce over crabs.

PREPARATION TIME: 5 minutes
COOKING TIME: 20 minutes
YIELD: 6 servings

Bell Island Crab Soufflé

Delicate yet flavorful, this soufflé makes a light luncheon dish for four people or a supper for three.

4	tablespoons butter
¼	cup flour
1	cup milk
3	eggs, separated
½	cup mayonnaise
½	teaspoon salt
1	teaspoon paprika
1	teaspoon minced parsley
4	scallions, minced
8	ounces crabmeat

1. Preheat oven to 400 degrees. Butter a 1½-quart soufflé dish.
2. Melt the butter in a medium saucepan. Stir in the flour and cook, stirring constantly over medium heat for 2 minutes. Slowly add the milk while stirring and cook until smooth and thick, about 2 minutes. Remove pan from heat and beat in the egg yolks one at a time.
3. Beat the egg whites with an electric mixer until stiff but not dry and set aside.
4. Gently blend the mayonnaise into the soufflé base and season with salt and paprika. Stir in the parsley, scallions and crabmeat. Gently fold in the beaten egg whites.
5. Pour into the prepared soufflé dish and bake in preheated oven until risen and lightly browned on top but still slightly wobbly when shaken, about 25 minutes. Serve immediately.

PREPARATION TIME: 30 minutes
COOKING TIME: 25 minutes
YIELD: 3-4 servings

Hot Crab Sandwiches

Serve these sandwiches for brunch or lunch or a light supper. The nice thing about this dish is it can be made ahead.

12	slices bread, crusts removed
2	cups crabmeat
6	slices American cheese
3	eggs, lightly beaten
2	cups milk
	salt and pepper to taste

1. In a greased 9 x 13" baking pan, place 6 slices of the bread. Spread crabmeat evenly over the bread slices. Top with cheese slices and place remaining bread on top of cheese.
2. Combine eggs, milk, salt and pepper and pour over sandwiches. Cover and refrigerate for at least 2 hours or for as long as overnight.
3. Preheat oven to 350 degrees. Bake uncovered for 30 minutes.

PREPARATION TIME: 15 minutes
COOKING TIME: 30 minutes
YIELD: 6 servings

Captain Henry of Bell Island is credited with being the first to cultivate oysters by spreading bushels of clean oyster shells in shallow water beds where the oyster larvae could attach and begin to grow. Today, huge mounds of oyster shells are visible along the Norwalk waterfront to be used for this underwater farming method.

Atlantic Coast Crab

A great recipe for a buffet.

1½   *cups diagonally sliced asparagus*
6   *ounces mushrooms, sliced*
¼   *cup chopped onion*
4   *tablespoons butter*
¼   *cup all-purpose flour*
½   *teaspoon curry powder*
¼   *teaspoon freshly ground black pepper*
½   *cup chicken stock*
1½   *cups half and half*
1   *pound cooked crabmeat*
¾   *cup grated cheddar cheese*
1   *can (3 ounces) crisp chow mein noodles*

1.   Blanch asparagus in rapidly boiling water for 1-2 minutes. Drain,
     then plunge into cold water. Drain again and set aside.
2.   In a large skillet, sauté the mushrooms and onion in the butter
     until soft. Sprinkle on flour, curry powder and pepper and con-
     tinue to cook and stir for one minute. Slowly add stock and half
     and half, stirring constantly to prevent lumping and simmer for
     one minute. Add crabmeat and reserved asparagus, transfer to
     a buttered 2-quart casserole and scatter cheese over the top.
     Recipe may be made ahead to this point. Cover and refrigerate,
     but bring back to room temperature before baking.
3.   Preheat oven to 375 degrees. Bake casserole uncovered for 20-
     30 minutes, or until cheese is melted and casserole is bubbly
     around the edges. Serve over the chow mein noodles or rice.

PREPARATION TIME: 45 minutes
COOKING TIME: 25 minutes
YIELD: 6 servings

Crabmeat Dewey

"Pop" Davis (Dr. Leland C. Davis) created this.

2   tablespoons butter
2   tablespoons flour
1¼   cups heavy cream
2   tablespoons unsalted butter for sauteeing
½   a green pepper, thinly sliced
1   cup mushrooms, sliced
¼   cup thinly sliced pimiento
1   pound Alaskan king crab, cooked
¼   cup cooking Sherry
     salt and pepper to taste

1.   Melt 2 tablespoons butter in a saucepan, stir in the flour and cook over low heat for about 2 minutes. Gradually stir in the cream and cook over low heat for 2 minutes until smooth and thick. Set aside.
2.   In a large skillet melt the other 2 tablespoons of butter and lightly sauté the green pepper and mushrooms. Add the pimiento, the crabmeat and the Sherry and stir in the reserved white sauce. Season to taste with salt and pepper. Serve immediately or keep warm in a covered casserole in the oven until ready to serve.

PREPARATION AND COOKING TIME: 40 minutes
YIELD: 4-6 servings

In 1880, the per capita consumption of oysters alone was three pounds per year. Today, Americans consume an average of only two pounds per person of all seafood combined. This pattern, however, is now on the upswing due to recent focus on seafood's nutritional value.

Crab and Spinach Casserole

Easily put together with ingredients you probably have on hand. It's also terrific using leftover cooked chicken.

2   packages frozen chopped spinach
1   cup finely chopped onions
1   pound crabmeat (or shrimp or scallops or cooked chicken)
1½   cups grated cheddar cheese
1   small can (6 ounces) tomato paste
½   pint (1 cup) sour cream
     dash nutmeg
     salt and pepper to taste

1.   Thaw spinach and squeeze out all excess liquid.
2.   Make 2 layers in a 2-quart casserole in the following order and using half of the ingredients for each layer: spinach, onions, crabmeat, cheese. Chill until ready to cook—up to 6 hours.
3.   When ready to bake, preheat oven to 325 degrees. Combine the tomato paste, sour cream, nutmeg and salt and pepper in a small bowl. Pour over the top of the casserole.
4.   Bake 35-45 minutes until bubbly and heated through.

BAKING TIME: 35-45 minutes
YIELD: 4-6 servings

Shad and salmon were once abundant and familiar fare on the dinnertables of 18th and 19th century Connecticut settlers. Thousands of barrels of shad were processed here during the Revolutionary War to feed the troops. Because of Connecticut's generosity of supplies during this war, it became known as the "Provision State".

Mary Lou's Crab and Shrimp

This is good with rice for a light supper and is delicious served on toast for a luncheon. It can also be served with crackers as an hors d'oeuvre.

1	*tablespoon butter*
2	*stalks celery, finely chopped*
½	*green pepper, finely chopped*
1	*teaspoon Worcestershire sauce*
¾	*cup mayonnaise*
1	*teaspoon lemon juice*
¾	*cup cooked chopped shrimp*
6	*ounces crabmeat*
¼	*teaspoon salt*
⅛	*teaspoon pepper*
½	*cup bread crumbs*
1	*tablespoon melted butter*

1. Preheat oven to 350 degrees.
2. Melt the butter in a skillet and sauté the celery and green pepper over medium heat for a few minutes until soft. Remove from heat and stir in Worcestershire and mayonnaise.
3. Sprinkle lemon juice over cooked shrimp and crab and add the seafood to the mayonnaise mixture. Season with salt and pepper. Transfer to a 1½-quart casserole, sprinkle with the crumbs and drizzle with melted butter. Bake in the preheated oven for 20 minutes or until it bubbles and is beginning to brown.

PREPARATION TIME: 20 minutes
COOKING TIME: 20 minutes
YIELD: 3-4 luncheon servings
2-3 dinner servings

Escabèche

An appealing version of a classic Portuguese dish.

2   *pounds halibut*
2   *cloves garlic*
1   *medium onion*
1   *carrot*
1   *each red, green and yellow bell peppers*
1   *cup water*
⅓   *cup white vinegar*
2   *tablespoons brown sugar*
1   *tablespoons cornstarch*
⅓   *cup oil*
       flour for dredging fish

1.   To prepare fish, remove all skin and bones and cut into one-inch
     chunks. Mince the garlic, chop the onion, and peel the carrot
     and cut into thin julienne strips. Seed the peppers and cut into
     thin strips.
2.   To prepare the sauce, in a small bowl mix together the water,
     vinegar, brown sugar and cornstarch. Set aside.
3.   Heat the oil in a large frying pan over medium-high heat. Lightly
     dredge the fish in the flour and fry in a single layer making sure
     fish is not sticking together so it can brown well on all sides. This
     may have to be done in two or three batches. When fish is
     browned, remove with a slotted spoon or tongs to a platter and
     keep warm in a slow oven.
4.   Add additional oil to pan, if necessary, to make two tablespoons.
     Add garlic and onions and sauté for two minutes over medium
     heat, scraping up any browned bits from the fish. Add carrots
     and peppers and sauté for five minutes, stirring occasionally.

Pour sauce ingredients into pan and cook, stirring, for five minutes until smooth and thickened. Pour sauce over fish and serve with rice.

PREPARATION AND COOKING TIME: 45 minutes
YIELD: 6 servings

Baked Fish with Sour Cream

This was first published in the contributor's own cookbook, *Forget-Me-Not Recipes*, which, unfortunately, is not currently in print. But we are lucky enough to have her recipe!

2   *pounds fillet of haddock, flounder, or other good white fish, fresh or frozen and thawed*
1   *cup sour cream*
1   *teaspoon lemon juice*
1   *teaspoon fresh parsley, chopped*
1   *shake garlic powder*
    Parmesan cheese
    paprika
    salt and pepper to taste

1.   Preheat oven to 325 degrees.
2.   Place fish in a greased shallow baking dish, about 8 x 10 inches. Combine sour cream, lemon juice, parsley, and garlic powder. Spread on top of fish. Sprinkle with Parmesan and paprika.
3.   Bake about 20 minutes until fish is cooked and top is browned.

PREPARATION TIME: 5 minutes
COOKING TIME: about 20 minutes
YIELD: 4-6 servings

★Fish Fondue de Rowayton

A perfect meal to have with good friends. The communal cooking process slows the pace and makes for a convivial evening.

4	cups bottled clam juice
2	cups dry white wine
2	cups water
1	large onion, sliced
1	stalk celery, chopped
1	large carrot, chopped
4	peppercorns
1	bay leaf
	salt to taste
¾	pound fillet of sole, cut in 1-inch bite sized pieces
¾	pound shrimp, shelled and deveined
1	pound bay scallops
½	pound lobster meat
	Tartar Sauce (recipe follows)
	Cocktail Sauce (recipe follows)
	Teriyaki Sauce (recipe follows)

1. To make the bouillon, combine in a large saucepan the clam juice, wine, water, onion, celery, carrot, peppercorns and bay leaf and bring to the boil. Simmer for 30 minutes, strain and discard solids. Add salt to taste.
2. Pour the bouillon into a fondue pot and heat with the flame beneath the pot. Have the seafood arranged on a platter in the center. Ask guests to spear chunks of fish and cook in the simmering bouillon until it tests done, about 1 minute each. Serve with accompanying dipping sauces.

PREPARATION AND COOKING TIME: 1¼ hours
YIELD: 6 servings

Tartar Sauce

½   cup mayonnaise
6   pitted green olives
1   small slice onion
2   sweet pickles
1   tablespoon capers

1.   Blend all ingredients together in a food processor or blender.

Cocktail Sauce

½   cup catsup
¼   cup chili sauce
2   teaspoons lemon juice
½   teaspoon lemon zest
½   teaspoon horseradish
½   teaspoon Worcestershire sauce

1.   Combine all ingredients in a small bowl.

Teriyaki Sauce

4   tablespoons butter
½   cup teriyaki sauce
2   teaspoons brown sugar
1   tablespoon lime juice
1   teaspoon grated ginger
1   garlic clove, minced

1.   Melt butter in a small saucepan. Add remaining ingredients and stir until sugar is dissolved.

Clementine's Flounder

Rich and delicious! This needs only plain rice and a steamed green vegetable such as beans for a super company meal.

6   *fillets of flounder or sole*
       about 3-4 cups fish stock for poaching (see note)
3   *tablespoons butter*
1   *shallot, minced*
1   *medium onion, minced*
1   *clove garlic, minced*
½   *pound mushrooms, minced*
6   *large sea scallops, diced*
       potpourri of herbs (parsley, tarragon, chives, chervil), about 1
       teaspoon each of fresh or ⅛ teaspoon each of dried
       salt and freshly ground pepper to taste
       Bechamel Sauce (recipe follows)
1   *ounce grated Parmesan cheese*

1. Preheat the broiler.
2. Place the fish fillets in a skillet and cover with stock. Poach gently for about 3-5 minutes until barely cooked. (The fish will be further cooked later.) Remove from stock with a slotted spoon and pour off all but 2 cups fish stock. Boil the 2 cups stock over medium-high heat to 1 cup. Reserve reduced stock for Bechamel sauce.
3. Heat the butter in a skillet and sauté the shallot and onion for about 3 minutes just until softened. Add the garlic and sauté one minute more. Add mushrooms and continue to sauté over medium-high heat, stirring until mushroom liquid has almost evaporated. Stir in the scallops and herbs and sauté about one minute until scallops are just cooked through. Add salt and pepper to taste.
4. Place the fish on a broiler-proof platter or pan and divide the mushroom mixture atop each fillet. Cover with Bechamel sauce

and sprinkle with cheese. Broil, about 4 inches from the heat source, for 1-2 minutes until lightly browned and heated through.

NOTE: Do not substitute bottled clam juice for the fish stock since it will become extremely salty when reduced. Any basic cookbook will give a recipe for fish stock and many fishmongers carry it in the freezer case.

Bechamel Sauce

¼   *cup (4 tablespoons) butter*
¼   *cup flour*
1   *cup fish stock reserved from poaching the fish*
½   *cup heavy cream*
3   *ounces grated Gruyere cheese (about 1 cup)*

1. In a heavy saucepan, melt the butter and blend in the flour. Cook, stirring constantly with a wooden spoon over medium-low heat. Gradually stir in the fish stock and then the cream until well blended. Slowly bring to a boil, stirring constantly, and then cook over low heat about one minute. Take the pan off the heat and stir in the cheese until melted.
2. Reserve sauce until ready to use.

NOTE: Sauce can be made early in the day up to adding the cheese and gently reheated to melt the cheese just before using.

PREPARATION AND COOKING TIME: 1 hour
YIELD: 6 servings

Fossils dredged up from Long Island Sound prove that the lobster appearance has remained the same for at least one hundred million years. The Pilgrim fathers considered lobster to be poorhouse fare and often donated it to charity. In colonial New England, a servant was considered lucky if he did not have to eat lobster more than twice a week! Today, commercial lobstermen land nearly two million pounds of lobster from Connecticut waters.

Fish En Papilotte

A dramatic show-stopper! The packets can be prepared early in the day and held in the refrigerator until baked.

10   *12-inch squares of baking parchment*
½   *pound (2 sticks) butter*
¾   *cup flour*
1½   *cups finely minced scallions*
3   *tablespoons chopped parsley*
3   *tablespoons dry white wine*
5   *egg yolks*
1½   *cups heavy cream*
½   *teaspoon white pepper*
¼   *teaspoon cayenne pepper*
2   *cups cooked shrimp, each shrimp cut in two pieces*
1½   *cups lump crabmeat*
10   *medium sole fillets*
     additional butter for parchment paper

1.   To form the papillotes, fold each square of parchment in half and cut into the shape of a half heart. When unfolded, parchment will be heart-shaped.
2.   In a large heavy saucepan, melt butter over medium heat. Gradually add flour and cook, stirring constantly for two minutes. Stir in scallions and parsley and cook for about 3 minutes, stirring frequently. Stir in the white wine.
3.   In a small bowl, whisk together the egg yolks and cream. Remove saucepan from heat. Add a small amount of the hot flour-butter mixture to the eggs and cream and then slowly whisk the remaining egg-cream mixture into the saucepan. Season with white pepper and cayenne.
4.   Lightly butter the inside of each papillote. Spoon a tablespoon or two of sauce into the center of each heart. Lay a sole fillet over sauce and layer some shrimp and crabmeat over sole. Spoon another tablespoon or so of sauce over seafood.

5. Fold down top half of heart over fish/sauce. To seal packets, begin at top rounded corner of the heart and fold in about ½ inch. Then make another fold overlapping with the first to seal. When you get to the bottom of the heart, twist the point twice so that steam cannot escape. (Recipe may be made ahead to this point and held for several hours in refrigerator.)
6. Preheat oven to 425 degrees. Arrange papillotes on a large baking sheet and bake for 15-20 minutes until parchment begins to brown. Check one for doneness of fish and do not overcook.
7. Serve on individual dinner plates, cutting each packet open at the table with scissors.

PREPARATION TIME: 45 minutes
COOKING TIME: 15-20 minutes
YIELD: 10 servings

Basic Broiled Bluefish

A simple, but most satisfying method of preparing fresh fillets.

1¼ pounds fresh bluefish fillets
3 tablespoons lemon juice
salt and pepper to taste
3 tablespoons butter or 4 strips bacon, cut in pieces
paprika
lemon wedges and parsley sprigs for garnish

1. Preheat the broiler. Butter a broiler proof pan large enough to hold the fish in a single layer.
2. Place the fish, skin side down on the pan. Sprinkle with lemon juice and salt and pepper to taste. Dot with butter or bacon and sprinkle with paprika.
3. Broil about 6 inches from the heat until the fish is cooked through, about 6 minutes.

PREPARATION TIME: 5 minutes
COOKING TIME: 6 minutes
YIELD: 4 servings

Broiled Haddock and Bananas

4   small or 1 large fillet of haddock
4   tablespoons unsalted butter
¼   cup lemon juice
¼   teaspoon crumbled dried tarragon or 1 teaspoon chopped fresh
    tarragon
⅛   teaspoon paprika
¼   teaspoon dry mustard
½   teaspoon salt
4   bananas

1. Preheat the broiler. Melt butter in a small saucepan and stir in
    lemon juice, tarragon, paprika, mustard and salt.
2. Place fish in broiler pan and brush with some of the butter mix-
    ture. Broil for 5-7 minutes until almost done. Peel banana, cut
    into thin slices and place on top of fish. Pour remaining butter
    mixture over bananas and broil for 2 minutes until bananas are
    lightly glazed. Serve immediately.

PREPARATION TIME: 10 minutes
COOKING TIME: 10 minutes
YIELD: 4 servings

---

*The song "Yankee Doodle" had its origins in Norwalk. In 1756, a brigade
of volunteers assembled at the home of Colonel Thomas Fitch where the
young recruits set out to assist the British during the French and Indian
War. Fitch's young sister stuck a feather into the hat band of each soldier
as he pulled out on his plow horse. The British, amused by the appearance
of the troops, wrote and sang the jingle in mockery. The rest is history.
Yankee Doddle became the rallying song for the colonial troops during the
Revolution and in 1979 became the official state song of Connecticut.*

Grilled Halibut Steaks with Orange and Coriander

An unusual and contemporary way of serving halibut.

2   *large halibut steaks (about 2 pounds total)*
3   *tablespoons safflower oil, divided*
2   *tablespoons unsalted butter, divided*
1   *shallot, minced*
1   *clove garlic, minced*
2   *ripe medium-size tomatoes, peeled, seeded and chopped*
⅔   *cup orange juice, freshly squeezed*
¼   *cup dry white wine*
     coarse salt and freshly ground pepper to taste
½   *cup fresh coriander leaves, chopped*

1. Preheat broiler or build a barbecue fire.
2. Wipe steaks dry with paper towels. Coat both sides with 2 tablespoons safflower oil and set aside.
3. Heat remaining safflower oil and 1 tablespoon butter in a skillet. Sauté the shallot and garlic for about one minute until softened. Add tomatoes and cook 3 minutes. Add orange juice and wine and reduce slightly over medium-high heat, about 5 minutes. Season to taste with salt and pepper and set aside.
4. Place steaks on broiling pan or on grill and cook about 4 minutes per side depending upon the thickness of the fish.
5. Bring the sauce to a boil. Remove from heat and stir in remaining 1 tablespoon butter and the coriander. Pour sauce over steaks and serve.

NOTE: Fresh coriander is also called cilantro or Chinese parsley.

PREPARATION TIME: 30 minutes
COOKING TIME: 8 minutes
YIELD: 4 servings

Down East Boiled Lobster

Serve this Maine dinner with plenty of melted butter for dipping, some garlic bread, a salad and blueberry pie. It's well worth hauling the sea water!

4   1½ *pound lobsters*
       sea water

1.   Purchase lobsters from a lobsterman or better yet take from your own pots.
2.   When ready to cook, fill a large pot half full of sea water. Bring the water to a full boil. (This will take a long time, especially if using COLD Maine water). While waiting, conduct lobster races on the kitchen floor, keeping the dogs out of the room! Add lobsters to the rapidly boiling water, return to a boil and cook about 10 minutes.
3.   Enjoy.

PREPARATION AND COOKING TIME: Approximately 1 hour
YIELD: 4 servings

Legend has it that George Washington, enroute to Cambridge to join the Continental Army passed through Bridgeport at supper time. He stopped at Pixlee Tavern where he feasted on the house specialty—oysters, fresh from the Long Island Sound, which were fried according to Mrs. Pixlee's original secret recipe.

As the story goes, General Washington had a difficult time getting served because the tavern was packed. He commented to a few men that his hungry horse would love some oysters. The tavern cleared out as the men scurried to feed a horse who would actually eat oysters. Washington was able to consume three quick platters of the succulent bivalves before the men returned inside, realizing that they had been tricked!

Lobster Newburg

A wonderful special occasion dish.

1½ *cups heavy cream*
3   *egg yolks*
     salt and freshly ground black pepper
     dash of cayenne pepper
3   *cups cooked lobster meat, cut into bite-sized chunks*
1   *tablespoon unsalted butter*
2   *tablespoons Cognac*
     Cooked rice or patty shells

1. Heat cream over low heat in a large heavy saucepan.
2. In a small bowl, lightly beat the egg yolks with a wire whisk. Slowly whisk the hot cream into the yolks, beating constantly. Return mixture to the saucepan, place over low heat, and cook, stirring almost constantly with a wooden spoon until custard thickens enough to coat the back of the spoon. Season with salt, pepper, and cayenne.
3. Add the lobster meat to the custard sauce and continue cooking on very low heat for about 5 minutes or until heated through. Add butter and Cognac and cook another minute until butter is melted.
4. Serve over rice or spoon into baked patty shells.

PREPARATION AND COOKING TIME: 30 minutes
YIELD: 4-6 servings

Lillian Hellman summered in a secluded house on Tavern Island in 1938 where she wrote her Broadway success, "The Little Foxes". In 1958, the colorful producer Billy Rose transformed the island into a showplace for his artworks. The remains of the statues of five Grecian maidens are still visible to boaters.

Lobster Thermidor

Deliciously rich way to stretch the extravagance of lobster. It's a lot of work, but worth it!

3   *lobsters, 1¼ pound each*
     fish stock for cooking lobsters
2   *shallots, chopped*
3   *tablespoons salted butter*
3   *tablespoons unsalted butter*
½   *cup dry white wine*
½   *teaspoon dry mustard, soaked 5 minutes in 1 tablespoon water*
2   *cups Mornay Sauce (recipe follows)*
     salt and freshly ground black pepper to taste
1   *tablespoon heavy cream, whipped*
½   *cup freshly grated Parmesan cheese*

1. Boil lobsters in fish stock for 5 minutes, reduce heat and simmer 15 minutes or until lobsters turn red. Remove lobsters from fish stock and when cool enough to handle, remove meat from claws and bodies, keeping the bodies intact. Cut the meat into bite-sized pieces and set aside.
2. Preheat the broiler.
3. In a saucepan, cook shallots in both kinds of butter for about 2 minutes until transparent. Add wine and reduce over high heat to one-fourth the original quantity. Add soaked mustard, Mornay Sauce and salt and pepper to taste. Heat through.
4. In a large saucepan, mix lobster meat with ⅔ of the sauce and gently heat through. Place a little of the remaining sauce in each of the reserved shells and then stuff with the lobster mixture. Blend whipped cream with the remaining sauce and spread over the tops of the lobsters. Sprinkle with Parmesan cheese.
5. Place lobsters on a broiler pan and broil, about 4 inches from the heat, for 1-2 minutes until browned.

Mornay Sauce

7   *tablespoons unsalted butter, divided*
4   *tablespoons flour*
1½   *cups light fish stock*
½   *cup heavy cream*
1   *teaspoon salt, or to taste*
1/16 *teaspoon ground white pepper*
½   *cup mixed freshly grated Gruyere and Parmesan cheeses*

1. In a one-quart heavy saucepan, melt 4 tablespoons of the butter. Remove from heat and whisk in flour. Cook, stirring over
medium-low heat, about one minute. Remove from heat and
whisk in stock. Bring to the boiling point, stirring, and then
remove from heat. Add cream, 3 tablespoons butter and the
cheeses.

PREPARATION TIME: 1½ hours
YIELD: 6 servings

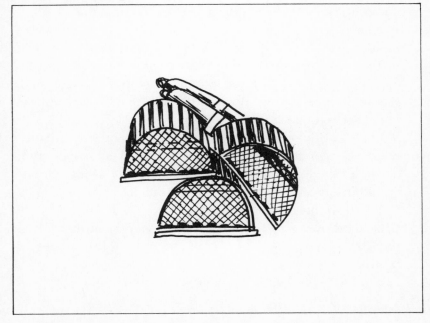

Baked Stuffed Lobster

An up-to-date tasty version of an old classic.

2   *lobsters, 2-2½ pounds apiece (one should be a female)*
1   *cup fresh bread crumbs*
1   *small red onion, finely chopped*
2   *garlic cloves, mashed*
1   *tablespoon capers*
1   *teaspoon fines herbes*
1   *cup sherry*
4   *tablespoons butter*

1. Preheat the oven to 325°.
2. Split the lobsters down the middle from head to tail. (You may steam them first for five minutes, if you wish, rather than attempt to split them alive!) Remove the green tomalley and the roe and set aside. Carefully remove the meat from the tails, making sure not to break the tail shells from the body. Chop the meat into small pieces.
3. Reduce the sherry to ½ cup over high heat. Reduce the heat to medium and add the butter, tomalley, roe, onion and garlic. Simmer until the onion is soft. Stir in the lobster meat and gently simmer for one minute. Remove the pan from the heat and stir in the herbs, bread crumbs, and capers.
4. Stuff the entire lobster shells (body and tail) with this mixture, mounding it on top. Place them on a cookie sheet being careful not to let the claws become detached. (At this point you may cover the lobsters and refrigerate them. Remove them from the fridge 30 minutes before cooking.)
5. Bake in the oven for 12 minutes. Place under the broiler 4″ from the heat source and broil for 3 minutes or until the crumbs are brown.
6. Serve with melted butter, lemon wedges and bibs!

PREPARATION TIME: 20 minutes
YIELD: 2 servings

Mussels in Italian Sauce

Serve as an entree over pasta if desired or as a delicious first course.

3-4 *quarts mussels*
4 *tablespoons unsalted butter*
3 *tablespoons olive oil*
2 *tomatoes, coarsely chopped*
5 *scallions, thinly sliced*
2 *cloves garlic, chopped*
pinch of oregano
pinch of rosemary
½ *cup chopped parsley*
½ *cup dry white wine*
salt and pepper to taste
additional chopped parsley as garnish

1. Scrub mussels, remove all barnacles and use pliers to pull off beards. (Do not use mussels that are already opened unless they close when you tap them with the back of a knife.)
2. In a 6-quart kettle, heat butter and olive oil and sauté tomatoes for 4 minutes. Add scallions, garlic, oregano, rosemary and parsley and sauté for a few minutes until soft. Add white wine, bring to a vigorous simmer, and add the mussels. Cover pot and simmer over medium-low heat until mussels are open and tender, 5-8 minutes. Taste sauce and season with salt and pepper.
3. Serve over pasta if desired or as a first course.

PREPARATION AND COOKING TIME: 45 minutes
YIELD: 4 servings as an entree
8 as a first course

Scalloped Oysters

This makes a good side dish to roast beef or turkey or can be a light main course.

4   *dozen shucked oysters (more if very small), drained and liq-*
        uor reserved
1   *cellophane packet Ritz crackers, crushed very fine*
½-¾   *cup half and half or cream*
8   *tablespoons unsalted butter*
        black pepper to taste

1. Preheat oven to 325 degrees.
2. Smear a 2-quart baking dish with butter. Place about 16 of the drained oysters on the bottom of the dish. Cover with a ¼-inch layer of the crushed crackers. Spoon over about 2 tablespoons of the oyster liquor. Pour about 3 tablespoons of cream over this layer and dot with about 2 tablespoons of butter. Sprinkle lightly with pepper. Repeat layering, ending with crackers. May be prepared ahead to this point and covered and refrigerated. Bring to room temperature before baking.
3. Bake uncovered in preheated oven for about 40 minutes, or until casserole is bubbly and golden on top.

PREPARATION TIME: 30 minutes
COOKING TIME: 40 minutes
YIELD: 4 servings

More oysters were shipped overseas from Long Island Sound than from any other place in the United States.
Oysters will not reproduce if the salinity of the water is too high. In Long Island Sound the salinity rate of 27-28 parts per thousand is ideal for the famous offshore beds from New Haven to Norwalk.

Oyster Festival Stuffing

½ pint fresh oysters or one 10-ounce can frozen oysters
1 package (6 ounces) Uncle Ben's long grain and wild rice mix
½ cup (8 tablespoons) butter
1½ cups sliced celery
1½ cups mushrooms, sliced
½ cup water
1 package (8 ounces) prepared herb stuffing
½ cup chopped parsley

1. At least two hours ahead of time, chop the oysters, turn them into a strainer set over a bowl and let drain. Reserve ½ cup of the oyster liquor.
2. Cook the rice mix according to package directions.
3. Melt the butter in a large skillet and sauté the celery and mushrooms for about 5 minutes.
4. Heat the reserved oyster liquor with the ½ cup water. Pour into the skillet. Add stuffing mix, cooked rice, oysters and parsley and toss all together gently to combine.
5. Spoon into turkey and roast.

PREPARATION AND COOKING TIME: 1 hour (excluding time to drain oysters)
YIELD: Enough for a 10-12 pound bird

Captain Adriaen Block skippered the Restless in 1614 on the first cruise on Long Island Sound by white men. He cruised by the Norwalk islands, passed the Quinipiac River at New Haven and explored the Connecticut River up to Hartford. He fished for salmon in the Thames and then sailed across the Sound to Montauk Point; from there he sailed on to the island which now bears his name.

Shrimp and Artichoke Casserole

4	(8½-ounce) cans artichoke hearts
1½-2	pounds cooked shrimp, cut in half if large
2	tablespoons butter for mushrooms
½	pound mushrooms, sliced
¼	cup flour for mushrooms
4	tablespoons butter for the sauce
4	tablespoons flour for the sauce
1	cup whipping cream
½	cup half and half
¼	cup dry Sherry
1	tablespoon Worcestershire sauce
	salt and pepper to taste
¼	cup grated Parmesan cheese
	sprinking of paprika

1. Drain artichokes and cut into small pieces. Place in the bottom of a 9 x 13″ baking dish. Arrange shrimp over artichokes.
2. In a large skillet, melt the 2 tablespoons of butter. Sauté the mushrooms in the butter over medium high heat for 2-3 minutes. Sprinkle flour over mushrooms and cook, stirring, for another 2 minutes. Scatter mushrooms over the shrimp in the baking dish.
3. In a large heavy saucepan, melt the 4 tablespoons of butter. Stir in the 4 tablespoons flour and cook, stirring, for 2 minutes. Add cream and half and half, stirring constantly. When thick and smooth, add the Sherry and Worcestershire and season to taste with salt and pepper. Pour sauce over the ingredients in the casserole, sprinkle top evenly with Parmesan cheese and dust with paprika. Casserole may be made ahead to this point and held covered in the refrigerator for up to 24 hours.
4. Preheat oven to 375 degrees. Bake casserole uncovered for 20-30 minutes until heated through and bubbly around the edges.

PREPARATION TIME: 35 minutes
COOKING TIME: 25 minutes
YIELD: 6 servings

Gregory's Honey Grilled Shrimp

This is a specialty of Gregory's Café in Fairfield. They say that chunks of vegetables can be added to the skewers with the shrimp. Serve the dish with any type of sweet fruit sauce, such as orange or raspberry, or creme fraiche and fresh fruit.

1   *cup dark corn syrup*
¼   *cup honey*
¼   *cup maple syrup*
¼   *cup orange juice*
20   *large shrimp, peeled and deveined*

1.   Combine the corn syrup, honey, maple syrup, and orange juice to make the marinade. Cover shrimp in marinade and let sit in the refrigerator at least 24 hours.
2.   Build a barbecue fire or preheat the broiler.
3.   Thread the shrimp on skewers and grill or broil about 2 minutes per side until shrimp turns pink.

PREPARATION TIME: 10 minutes (excluding marinating time)
YIELD: 4 servings

Bourbon Street Blackened Redfish

This is the way Chef Anthony Jucha at Bourbon Street Restaurant in Stamford prepares a Cajun specialty. The recipe yields one serving, but there is enough spice mix and butter to prepare about 4 servings. Simply repeat the cooking procedure.

Spice Mix

¼   teaspoon dried oregano
¼   teaspoon dried basil
¼   teaspoon dried tarragon
¼   teaspoon caraway seeds
¼   teaspoon dried red pepper flakes
¼   teaspoon garlic salt
¼   teaspoon onion powder
¼   teaspoon cayenne pepper
¼   teaspoon white pepper
¼   teaspoon black pepper
½   teaspoon paprika
⅛   teaspoon dried thyme
1   teaspoon kosher salt

Fish

8   ounce fillet of red fish or any other firm textured fish per portion
       about 2 tablespoons melted butter per portion

1.   To prepare the spice mix, crush all ingredients together with a mortar and pestle or grind in a spice grinder or mini-food processor. You will have about 4 teaspoons spice mix.
2.   To prepare the fish, preheat the oven to 350 degrees. Heat a cast iron skillet until extremely hot and nearly smoking. Dip the fish in the melted butter and then coat with an even layer (about 1 teaspoon) of the spice mixture.

3.   Sear the fish for about 30 seconds per side in the hot skillet and then transfer to a baking dish and place in the oven for 8-12 minutes until the fish is just cooked through.

PREPARATION TIME: 10 minutes
COOKING TIME: 12 minutes
YIELD: one serving

Fried Sesame Scrod

Mrs. Lee, the contributor's former maid, gave her this recipe.

1½   *pound scrod cut into 6 serving pieces*
2   *tablespoons soy sauce*
2   *tablespoons toasted sesame seeds*
⅛   *teaspoon black pepper*
2   *tablespoons minced scallions*
2   *tablespoons sesame oil*
2   *tablespoons vegetable oil*

1.   Rinse and pat scrod dry.
2.   Combine soy sauce, sesame seeds, pepper and minced scallions in a shallow dish.
3.   Heat the two oils in a large skillet. Dip fish in sesame-soy mixture and fry in the skillet over medium heat until fish is nicely browned and cooked through, 6-8 minutes.

PREPARATION AND COOKING TIME: 20 minutes
YIELD: 4-6 servings

Queen Victoria received a barrel of choice Norwalk oysters sent as a gift by the local oystermen. The oysters were "sandpapered and polished so that they could be handled with kid gloves".

Poached Salmon

This recipe will work with any size salmon depending upon how many guests you wish to serve. In this unusual method, the fish is "poached" in aluminum foil atop a gas grill.

　　heavy duty aluminum foil
1　*whole salmon (about 6 pounds), cleaned and scaled and*
　　prepared for poaching (the fishmonger will do this)
1-2　*cups white wine or as needed*
3　*tablespoons chopped parsley*
1　*bunch scallions, chopped*
　　salt and pepper
　　lemon wedges, if serving hot
　　Dill Sauce, if serving cold (recipe follows)

1.　Preheat a gas grill. Have ready a piece of heavy duty aluminum foil large enough to easily enclose the fish and form the poaching "pan".
2.　Place the fish in the center of the foil and fold up the sides. Add enough wine to come half-way up the fish. Sprinkle with the parsley, scallions, salt and pepper.
3.　Pull foil loosely around fish and seal well by crimping. Place on gas grill. Adjust heat to low to allow fish to gently poach. Open the packet and baste frequently with a bulb baster. Cook for about 30 minutes or until the fish is cooked through.
4.　Serve hot with lemon wedges or cold with Dill Sauce.

Dill Sauce

1	cup Hellmann's mayonnaise
½	cup minced dill pickle
2	scallions, minced
1	teaspoon dried dillweed
¼	teaspoon celery seed
½	teaspoon Lea and Perrins Worcestershire Sauce
2	teaspoons lemon juice

1. Combine all ingredients. Chill several hours.

PREPARATION TIME: 10 minutes
COOKING TIME: 30 minutes
YIELD: 8 servings

Baked Salmon Steaks

Serve this nice light fish with a baked potato and buttered broccoli.

2	salmon steaks about 1 inch thick
2	teaspoons olive oil
2	teaspoons coarse grain mustard (I use Pommery)
	juice from ½ lemon

1. Preheat oven to 350 degrees.
2. Pour olive oil into a small baking dish. Coat the salmon steaks top and bottom with the mustard and place them in the baking dish. Sprinkle lemon juice over fish.
3. Bake in preheated oven 20-30 minutes or until fish tests done.

PREPARATION TIME: 5 minutes
COOKING TIME: 25-35 minutes
YIELD: 2 servings

Salmon Steaks En Papillote

When you open these little foil packages, wonderful aromas will emerge to tantalize your guests. The packets can be assembled a few hours ahead and refrigerated. Add a couple of minutes to the baking time.

5   tablespoons butter, divided
2   medium carrots, julienned
1   medium onion, julienned
12 medium mushrooms, julienned
1   teaspoon chopped fresh tarragon
    salt and pepper to taste
4   (14 inch) circles of aluminum foil
2   tablespoons oil
4   small salmon steaks (6 ounces each)
4   whole sprigs fresh tarragon
8   tablespoons white wine
4   tablespoons chicken stock

1. Melt 4 tablespoons of the butter in a skillet and sauté the carrots and onion over medium-low heat until softened, about 5 minutes. Add mushrooms and cook 2-3 minutes. Add chopped tarragon and cook one minute. Season with salt and pepper and let cool.
2. Brush the foil circles with some of the oil. Spread the vegetables equally on one half of each circle. Cut each salmon steak into 5 or 6 pieces or place whole atop the vegetables. Place the tarragon sprigs atop the salmon. Dot with remaining 1 tablespoon butter and sprinkle each serving with 2 tablespoons wine and 1 tablespoon chicken stock.
3. Seal each papillote by bringing top half of circle over the bottom half and sealing edges by crimping.
4. Preheat oven to 475 degrees.
5. Brush baking sheet with oil and preheat sheet for 2-3 minutes. Place foil packages on baking sheet so that they are not touch-

ing. Bake 5-8 minutes until salmon is just cooked through and foil is puffed. Serve immediately.

PREPARATION TIME: 30 minutes
COOKING TIME: 5-8 minutes
YIELD: 4 servings

Fillet of Salmon with Mustard Sauce

Serve this sophisticated dish for a special occasion with boiled new potatoes and steamed green beans.

2   *pounds salmon fillets*
4   *tablespoons butter, melted*
       juice of 1 lemon
4   *shallots, finely chopped*
½   *cup white wine*
⅔   *cup heavy cream*
1½   *teaspoons Dijon-style mustard*
1½   *teaspoons salt, or to taste*
1   *teaspoon freshly ground pepper*

1.   Preheat the oven to 400 degrees. Arrange the salmon in a single layer in a large baking dish. Drizzle the butter and lemon juice over the fish. Place the baking dish in the oven and cook, uncovered, for 15 minutes.
2.   In a small saucepan, simmer the shallots and wine together over low heat until wine has evaporated and shallots are tender, about 8 minutes. Stir in cream, mustard, salt and pepper.
3.   Pour sauce over fish, return to the oven and cook for an additional 5 minutes, or until fish is glazed, but not browned.

PREPARATION AND COOKING TIME: 35 minutes
YIELD: 6 servings

Salmon Steaks in Lettuce Leaves

The lettuce leaves protect the fish from the heat of the grill and help prevent it from falling apart.

⅓   *cup lemon juice*
½   *cup olive or vegetable oil*
¼   *cup soy sauce*
3   *tablespoons chopped parsley*
3   *tablespoons minced green onions*
½   *teaspoon fennel seeds*
6   *salmon steaks, approximately 6 ounces each*
12 *large Romaine lettuce leaves*

1. Combine lemon juice, oil, soy sauce, parsley, green onions and fennel seed in a glass dish. Add fish, turning to coat completely with the marinade and let marinate at room temperature for 1 hour.
2. Prepare a barbecue fire.
3. To form the packets, lay a lettuce leaf on the work surface, place a salmon steak on the lettuce, and spoon some marinade over it. Fold the lettuce up over the salmon, wrap with a second leaf, and tie the whole thing up like a package using kitchen twine. Brush packets lightly with oil.
4. Grill about 5 inches above medium-hot coals for 15-20 minutes, turning a few times to help prevent scorching. Check one packet for doneness of fish. Meanwhile, heat remaining marinade in a saucepan for 2 minutes. To serve, snip twine with scissors or knife and remove top leaf of lettuce. Pass sauce to spoon over salmon.

PREPARATION TIME: 20 minutes (excluding marinating time)
COOKING TIME: 15 minutes
YIELD: 6 servings

Scalloped Scallops

½   cup (8 tablespoons) butter
1   cup Pepperidge Farm herbed stuffing
½   cup soft bread crumbs
1-1½ pounds sea scallops
⅔   cup milk or light cream

1. Preheat oven to 350 degrees. Melt butter, add Pepperidge Farm stuffing and bread crumbs and toss to combine. Spread about half the bread crumbs in the bottom of a shallow 1½-2 quart baking dish. Spread scallops over the crumbs and top with the remaining crumbs. Pour milk or cream over all.
2. Bake uncovered in the preheated oven for about 25 minutes.

PREPARATION TIME: 5 minutes
COOKING TIME: 25 minutes
YIELD: 4 servings

Captain Walt's Cape Scallops

1   pound sea scallops
1   cup flour
2   eggs, lightly beaten
1   cup fine dry bread crumbs
      Crisco oil for frying

1. Rinse scallops and pat dry. Dredge in the flour, shaking off the excess, then dip in the egg, and then roll in the bread crumbs. Set aside on a rack or baking sheet for 30 minutes.
2. Heat about ¾-inch of oil in a large heavy skillet at least 2 inches deep. When oil is hot, cook the scallops, one layer at a time, turning frequently with tongs, until golden brown on all sides, about 8 minutes. Serve with tartar sauce and lemon wedges.

PREPARATION TIME: 10 minutes (excluding resting time)
COOKING TIME: 15 minutes
YIELD: 3-4 servings

Bay Scallops with Monterey Jack Cheese

A nice easy scallop recipe that takes on a certain elegance when presented in individual ramekins. This recipe is for two but can easily be doubled.

14   *ounces bay scallops*
     salt and pepper to taste
2   *tablespoons butter*
2   *tablespoons Marsala*
6   *ounces Monterey Jack cheese, cut into six slices*
2   *tablespoons crushed herb seasoned croutons*

1. Preheat oven to 500 degrees. Butter two individual gratin dishes.
2. Divide scallops between the two dishes and sprinkle lightly with salt and pepper. Dot with butter and pour one tablespoon Marsala over each serving. Cover scallops with the slices of cheese and sprinkle the tops of the ramekins with the crumbs. Bake in the preheated oven for 10 minutes until tops are browned, cheese is melted, and scallops are cooked.

PREPARATION TIME: 15 minutes
COOKING TIME: 10 minutes
YIELD: 2 servings

If you're a fisherman and enjoy gardening, here's a trick the Pilgrims learned from the Indians. Save your trash fish in the freezer; at planting time drop one into the soil underneath plants such as tomatoes. Watch those plants grow!

Fish Steaks with Salmoriglo Sauce

The contributor got this recipe off the back of a package of paper towels one summer on Nantucket—if you can believe it! It's become a family favorite.

3   tablespoons lemon juice
¼   teaspoon salt
1   teaspoon crushed oregano
¼   cup olive oil
    fresh pepper to taste
2   pounds swordfish or salmon cut into half-inch thick steaks

1. Preheat the broiler or fire up the grill. In a small bowl, blend lemon juice, salt and oregano. Add the oil gradually, stirring constantly with a whisk. Season with a lot of fresh pepper.
2. When broiler or grill is quite hot, place the fish quite close to the source of heat as it must cook quickly. Cook about 2 minutes per side. Do not overcook or fish becomes dry and tough. Transfer to a warm platter. Whisk sauce to recombine, spoon it over the fish and serve.

PREPARATION TIME: 5-10 minutes (excluding building the barbecue fire)
COOKING TIME: 5 minutes
YIELD: 4 servings

Oystermen who lived along the Five Mile River in Rowayton often turned their seaport homes into boarding homes for summer visitors. This allowed a little extra cash for their families to enjoy a few comforts. Many artists summered in Rowayton attracted by its charm and scenic beauty.

Southport Seafood Casserole

A good party dish.

3   *tablespoons butter*
3   *tablespoons flour*
2   *cups light cream or half and half*
¼   *cup Sherry*
     salt and pepper to taste
¼   *teaspoon celery salt, or to taste*
2   *tablespoons butter for sautéing vegetables*
½   *pound mushrooms, sliced*
½   *cup chopped green pepper*
1   *pound cooked shrimp*
½   *pound sea scallops, cut in half*
1   *cup cooked crabmeat*
2   *tablespoons chopped pimiento*
2   *tablespoons chopped parsley*
½   *cup bread crumbs*
2   *tablespoons melted butter*

1. To make the cream sauce, melt 3 tablespoons of butter in a large
    heavy saucepan, stir in the flour, and cook, stirring with a
    wooden spoon, for 2 minutes. Stir in the cream and cook over
    medium-high heat until thick and bubbly. Add the Sherry and
    season to taste with salt, pepper and celery salt.
2. In a large skillet, melt 2 tablespoons of butter. Sauté the mush-
    rooms and green pepper for 5 minutes. Add them to the cream
    sauce along with the shrimp, scallops and crabmeat. Add
    pimiento and parsley and stir gently to combine. Turn into a
    buttered 2-quart casserole, sprinkle with the crumbs, and driz-
    zle with the melted butter. May be made ahead to this point,
    wrapped, and refrigerated for up to several hours.

3.   Preheat oven to 375 degrees. Bake casserole uncovered for 25-35 minutes, until heated through and top is browned.

PREPARATION TIME: 40 minutes
COOKING TIME: 30 minutes
YIELD: 8-10 servings

Baked Fish with Dill Sauce

4   *fish fillets (sole, flounder, scrod, etc.) about 6 ounces each*
8   *tablespoons butter*
1   *tablespoon minced onion*
1   *tablespoon chopped fresh dill or ¾ teaspoon dried*
1   *teaspoon sugar*
¼   *teaspoon thyme*
¼   *teaspoon salt*
⅛   *teaspoon pepper*
1   *cup sour cream*
     dill sprigs for garnish, if available

1.   Preheat oven to 375 degrees. Place fish in a single layer in a buttered baking dish.
2.   Melt the butter in a saucepan. Remove from heat and stir in all remaining ingredients except the dill sprigs for garnish. Spread sauce over fillets.
3.   Bake uncovered in preheated oven for about 15 minutes until fish tests done. Garnish with reserved dill sprigs before serving.

PREPARATION TIME: 15 minutes
COOKING TIME: 15 minutes
YIELD: 4 servings

★Seafood Mornay Casserole

1½ *cups white wine*
1½ *cups water*
1   *pound scallops*
1   *pound shrimp, shelled and deveined*
1   *pound scrod, cut in chunks*
6   *tablespoons butter*
6   *tablespoons flour*
3   *cups light cream*
1   *cup grated white cheddar cheese*
½   *cup Parmesan cheese*
½   *cup grated Swiss cheese*
     salt and black pepper to taste
1   *cup bread crumbs*

1. Combine wine and water in a large saucepan and bring to a boil.
    Poach the seafood in the simmering liquid for 3-5 minutes until
    cooked through. Set aside.
2. In a clean saucepan, melt the butter, stir in the flour, and cook
    over medium heat for 3 minutes, stirring constantly. Slowly add
    the cream and cook until thick. Remove sauce from the heat and
    add in the grated cheeses, stirring until melted. Season with
    black pepper and salt to taste. Fold the seafood into the sauce
    and transfer to a buttered 3-quart casserole. May be prepared
    ahead to this point and held in the refrigerator for several hours.
3. Preheat oven to 350 degrees. Sprinkle top of casserole with bread
    crumbs and bake in preheated oven for 35-40 minutes until top
    is browned and sauce is bubbly. Serve with white rice or in patty
    shells.

PREPARATION TIME: 35 minutes
COOKING TIME: 35 minutes
YIELD: 8 servings

Foiled Baked Fish

Make these packets early in the day and bake just before serving.

2   *fillets of fish (sole, haddock, etc.) about 6 ounces each*
2   *tablespoons butter*
2   *tablespoons white wine*
1   *teaspoon lemon juice*
1   *small onion, thinly sliced*
1   *carrot, peeled and cut into julienne pieces*
      paprika
      salt and pepper to taste
2   *10-inch sheets of foil*

1. Preheat oven to 400 degrees.
2. Rinse fillets and place each on a sheet of foil. Place 1 tablespoon of butter on each piece of fish, then sprinkle with wine and lemon juice. Arrange onion slices and julienned carrot over the top, sprinkle with paprika, salt and pepper and fold in edges of foil and crimp to seal.
3. Place on a rimmed baking sheet and bake in preheated oven for about 15 minutes. Check one of the packets to see whether fish is opaque. Place packets on individual plates and open with scissors at the table.

PREPARATION TIME: 15 minutes
COOKING TIME: 15 minutes
YIELD: 2 servings

Oysters and clams take an average of four to five years to reach commercial size. A one-pound lobster is seven years old. Shell-fishermen can control the growth rate of clams and oysters by transferring their crop to deeper waters which retards their growth. They can protect themselves from flooding the seafood market and thus lowering their profits.

Mexican Fish Kebabs

2½-3 *pounds fish and/or shellfish (swordfish, tuna, monkfish, large*
        shrimp or sea scallops)
½   *cup oil*
¼   *cup lime juice*
2   *teaspoons white wine vinegar*
2   *finely chopped jalapeño peppers*
2   *tablespoons chopped cilantro*
1   *tablespoon finely chopped garlic*
½   *teaspoon salt*
2   *red bell peppers, seeded and cut in 1½-inch cubes*

1. Cut the fish into 1½-inch chunks. Peel and devein shrimp, if
    using.
2. Combine oil, lime juice, vinegar, jalapeños, cilantro, garlic and
    salt in a bowl, add seafood and marinate for 1-2 hours.
3. Build a barbecue fire. Soak mesquite chips, if available, for 20
    minutes, and toss on the fire just before cooking. Alternate fish,
    shellfish (if using) and red pepper chunks on skewers, prefera-
    bly bamboo ones that have been soaked for 1 hour.
4. Grill kebabs over medium-hot fire for about 3 minutes per side,
    or until fish tests done. Serve with green salsa (La Victoria is fine)
    and buttered tortillas.

PREPARATION TIME: 30 minutes (excluding marinating time)
COOKING TIME: 10 minutes
YIELD: 6 as an entree
          10 as an appetizer

Seafood Barnum

This is a recipe from Chef Greg Loundes at J.F. O'Connell's Pub in Bridgeport.

2	*cups chicken stock*
1	*cup raw rice*
2	*tablespoons olive oil*
½	*pound scallops*
½	*pound shrimp, peeled and deveined*
½	*pound sole*
1	*pound halibut*
1	*cup flour*
1	*cup clam juice, divided*
¼	*cup white wine*
1	*stick (8 tablespoons) butter*
1	*tablespoon chopped garlic*
¾	*cup chopped clams*
2	*tablespoons parsley*

1. Bring chicken stock to the boil, add rice and stir. Cover and cook 20 minutes on low heat. Set aside.
2. In a large sauté pan, heat olive oil. Dredge scallops, shrimp, sole and halibut in flour, shaking off excess. Sauté each seafood separately in the oil until golden and cooked through. Time will vary according to fish. Remove all shellfish and fish from sauté pan and add half of the clam juice, the wine, and the butter. Heat and stir to form a sauce.
3. In a separate pan, heat together the remaining clam juice, garlic, and chopped clams. Mix with the rice.
4. To serve, lay rice on a large plate, arrange seafood over top and pour butter sauce over all. Garnish with chopped parsley.

PREPARATION TIME: 45 minutes
YIELD: 6-8 servings

Vegetable Fish Packets

Strips of beautiful vegetables add color and crunch to this version of fish cooked "en papillote." The sole steams in its own juices, its wonderful aromas released when the packages are opened at the table.

4	*sole or flounder fillets*
	salt and pepper to taste
8	*8-inch squares of foil*
	butter for foil
4	*tablespoons butter*
2	*carrots, peeled and cut in julienne slices*
2	*ribs celery, cut in julienne slices*
8	*mushrooms, sliced*
2	*scallions, cut in julienne slices*
1	*tablespoon minced shallots*
¼	*cup cream*

1. Lightly butter four of the sheets of foil. Sprinkle the fish fillets lightly with salt and pepper and lay one fillet on each of the four pieces of foil.
2. Melt the 4 tablespoons of butter in a large skillet. Add the vegetables and sauté over medium heat for 2 minutes. Add the cream and cook over high heat until most of the liquid is evaporated, about 3-4 minutes. Vegetables should remain crisp.
3. Divide vegetable mixture evenly over each sole fillet. Cover each with remaining sheets of foil and crimp edges to seal tightly so that steam cannot escape. Packets may be prepared up to several hours ahead to this point and refrigerated.
4. Preheat oven to 325 degrees. Place packets on a rimmed baking sheet and bake in the preheated oven for 10-12 minutes, or until fish tests done when checked. Serve packets on individual plates and open with scissors at the table.

PREPARATION TIME: 30 minutes
COOKING TIME: 10-12 minutes
YIELD: 4 servings

"The Ritz" Seafood Casserole

A good do-ahead casserole for a large group.

1   *package (6½ ounce) long grain and wild rice*
1½   *pounds medium shrimp, peeled and deveined*
10   *ounces cooked lobster or crabmeat*
¼   *cup (4 tablespoons) butter*
1   *medium onion, chopped*
½   *pound fresh mushrooms, sliced*
1   *cup chopped celery*
1   *green pepper, seeded and chopped*
     2-ounce jar pimientos, chopped
1   *teaspoon salt, or to taste*
½   *cup slivered almonds*
2   *cans undiluted cream of mushroom soup*
¼   *cup milk*
½   *cup Sherry*

1. Cook rice according to package directions.
2. Meanwhile, cook the shrimp in a large pot of lightly salted boiling water for 1-2 minutes, or until they turn pink. Drain, combine with the lobster or crabmeat and set aside.
3. Melt the butter in a large skillet and sauté the onion, mushrooms, celery and green pepper over medium-high heat for about 10 minutes. Stir in pimientos, salt, and almonds.
4. In a large mixing bowl, stir together the cream of mushroom soup, milk and Sherry. Add the rice, the seafood and the vegetable mixture and stir to combine. Turn into a lightly greased large casserole (approximately 9" x 13" or larger).*
5. Preheat oven to 350 degrees. Cover loosely with foil and bake casserole for about 45 minutes until heated through and bubbly around the edges.

*May be prepared ahead to this point. Cover and refrigerate for up to 24 hours. Remove from refrigerator at least 1 hour before baking.

PREPARATION TIME: 45 minutes
COOKING TIME: 45 minutes
YIELD: 8-12 servings

★Southern Shrimp Boil

This recipe comes originally from an old Florida family. Serve on a newspaper-covered table, preferably outdoors. Just invite people to roll up their sleeves and dig in! It's wonderful, messy fun.

6	*pounds unshelled shrimp*
8	*cups water*
1	*tablespoon caraway seed*
1	*tablespoon whole black peppercorns*
1	*tablespoon pickling spice*
1	*teaspoon cayenne pepper*
1	*bay leaf*
1	*teaspoon dry mustard*
2	*teaspoons salt*
3	*sprigs parsley*
	top leaves of one bunch of celery
	Seasoned Butter Sauce (recipe follows)

1. Wash the shrimp well in cold water and set aside.
2. In a large pot combine the water, caraway, peppercorns, pickling spice, cayenne, bay leaf, mustard, salt, parsley and celery leaves. Bring to the boil, reduce heat and simmer for 20 minutes. Add the shrimp, return to the boil and cook for about 5 minutes until shrimp shells have turned pink. Drain and dump in the middle of your table which has been covered with newspaper. Peel shrimp with your hands and dip in the sauce before eating. Serve with beer or lemonade.

Seasoned Butter Sauce

½   *pound butter*
     juice of 2 large lemons
2   *tablespoons soy sauce*
1   *tablespoon Worcestershire*
1   *tablespoon tarragon vinegar*
1   *teaspoon salt*
     several dashes of Tabasco, or to taste

1.   In a small saucepan melt the butter with all other ingredients. Serve in small bowls for dipping shrimp.

PREPARATION AND COOKING TIME: 40 minutes
YIELD: 6 servings

Stew Leonard's Teriyaki Fish Kebabs

1½   *pounds swordfish, shark, salmon, or tuna steaks*
3   *tablespoons lime juice*
3   *tablespoons soy sauce*
1   *teaspoon sugar*
2   *tablespoons oriental sesame oil*
2   *green peppers*

1.   Trim all skin and any bones from the fish. Cut into 1½ inch cubes. Place in a glass or ceramic bowl.
2.   Mix the lime juice, soy sauce and sugar together. Stir in the sesame oil. Pour this mixture over the fish and toss lightly to coat all sides. Allow to marinate for 30 minutes.
3.   Core and seed the green peppers and cut into 1½ inch squares.
4.   Preheat barbecue grill or broiler.
5.   Arrange fish on skewers alternating with pieces of green pepper. Grill, turning skewers to cook all sides, until fish is cooked through and browned, about 15 minutes. Do not overcook.

PREPARATION TIME: 30 minutes
YIELD: 4 servings

Dan's Louisana Shrimp Casserole

Just add a salad for a simple dinner.

8   tablespoons butter or margarine
1   cup chopped onions
3   cloves garlic, minced
1   cup chopped celery
1   cup chopped green pepper
1   cup chopped shallots or scallions
⅓   cup chopped parsley
1   small can chopped pimientos with juice
1   pound cooked shrimp
1   can mushroom soup
1   can cheddar cheese soup
2   slices toasted bread cut in cubes
2   cups cooked rice
½   teaspoon salt, or to taste
½   teaspoon black pepper
1-2   tablespoons liquid hot pepper sauce (use to taste)
½   cup Parmesan cheese
½   cup bread crumbs

1. In a large skillet, melt the butter and sauté the onions, garlic, celery and green pepper for about 5 minutes until tender. Add the parsley, shallots or scallions, and pimiento and stir in the shrimp and the soups. Add bread cubes and rice and season with the salt, pepper and liquid hot pepper sauce. Stir gently to mix.
2. Turn into a greased 2-3 quart casserole and sprinkle with the Parmesan and bread crumbs. May be made ahead to this point. Cover with foil and refrigerate. Bring back to room temperature before baking.

3.   Preheat oven to 350 degrees. Bake the casserole covered for 25-30 minutes until heated through. Remove foil cover for last few minutes of baking time so top can brown lightly.

PREPARATION TIME: 30 minutes
COOKING TIME: 30 minutes
YIELD: 6 servings

Greek Shrimp

1   *cup raw rice*
1½   *pounds large shrimp, peeled and deveined*
¼   *cup lemon juice*
¼   *cup whipped butter*
1   *clove garlic, minced*
½   *cup chopped scallions, including tops*
1½   *large ripe tomatoes, peeled and cut into wedges (or substitute 3 canned plum tomatoes when fresh are not in season)*
½   *teaspoon oregano*
     black pepper to taste
½   *pound crumbled feta cheese*
⅓   *cup cream sherry*

1.   Cook the rice according to package directions.
2.   Sprinkle the shrimp with the lemon juice and set aside. Melt the butter in a large skillet and sauté the garlic, scallions and tomatoes, stirring often, for about 5 minutes. Add shrimp to skillet, along with oregano, pepper, cheese and sherry and simmer uncovered 3-4 minutes, until shrimp has turned pink. Serve over rice.

PREPARATION AND COOKING TIME: 40 minutes
YIELD: 4 servings

Chicken and Shrimp Tchoupitoulas

Named after the oldest street in New Orleans where chicken and shrimp have long been a favorite combination. The recipe comes to us from Water Street Restaurant in South Norwalk.

5	*tablespoons butter, divided*
4	*tablespoons flour*
1	*pound shrimp, peeled and deveined*
1	*boneless and skinless chicken breast, cut into bite-sized pieces*
½	*pound mushrooms, sliced*
2	*tablespoons finely minced garlic*
¼	*cup white wine*
4	*artichoke hearts (canned or cooked), quartered*
4	*tablespoons chopped pimientos*
½	*cup scallions, thinly sliced*
2	*tablespoons chopped parsley*
1	*cup shrimp stock or clam juice*
¼	*cup lemon juice*
	salt, cayenne pepper, pepper and Worcestershire sauce to taste
	cooked rice

1. To make the roux, melt 2 tablespoons of the butter in a heavy saucepan, stir in the flour and cook, stirring, about 2 minutes until mixture is smooth.

2. In a skillet, sauté the shrimp, chicken, and mushrooms in the remaining 3 tablespoons butter, stirring constantly until shrimp lose their translucence. Add garlic, cook briefly, and then add wine and cook at high heat until wine evaporates. Add artichoke hearts, pimientos, scallions and parsley. Cook for one minute to blend and then add stock and lemon juice. Add the cooked roux

and stir until thickened. Add the seasonings and blend well.

3. Serve over the cooked rice.

PREPARATION TIME: 30 minutes
COOKING TIME: 10 minutes
YIELD: 4 servings

★Garlic Broiled Shrimp

The mother-in-law of one of our testers pronounced this "pure heaven!"

2 *pounds large fresh shrimp, peeled and deveined (see note)*
½ *cup (8 tablespoons) butter, melted*
½ *cup olive oil*
¼ *cup fresh parsley, chopped*
1 *tablespoon chopped green onion*
3 *cloves garlic, minced*
1½ *tablespoons fresh lemon juice*
Freshly ground black pepper

1. Combine butter, olive oil, parsley, green onion, garlic and lemon juice in a large shallow dish. Add shrimp, tossing to coat. Cover and marinate at least 30 minutes, stirring occasionally. Set oven to broil.
2. Place shrimp on broiler pan and broil 4 inches from the heat source for 3-4 minutes. Turn and broil for another 3 minutes or until done. Top with a few turns of the peppermill and serve with the pan drippings with pasta or rice.

NOTE: I prefer to use shrimp that have been peeled but with the tails left on and split (or "butterflied") up the back. You can ask your fish market to do this for you.

PREPARATION TIME: 40 minutes (including marinating time)
COOKING TIME: 7 minutes
YIELD: 4-6 servings

★Spicy Prawns

The heat comes from the whole dried chiles. Eat them carefully!

1½ *pounds shrimp, shelled and deveined*

1   *cup cold water*
2   *teaspoons cornstarch*
1   *tablespoon cold water*
1   *egg white, beaten slightly*
8   *dried red chiles*
1   *teaspoon cornstarch*
2   *teaspoons cold water*
1   *tablespoon soy sauce*
2   *teaspoons dry Sherry*
1½ *teaspoons honey*
1   *teaspoon white vinegar*
3   *tablespoons oil*
2   *scallions, chopped*
1   *teaspoon grated fresh ginger*
2   *cloves garlic, minced*

1. Put shrimp in cold water and let stand 5 minutes. Drain and pat dry.
2. Combine cornstarch, 1 tablespoon water, and egg white in a bowl. Add shrimp and stir to coat evenly. Let sit for 30 minutes.
3. Meanwhile, break tops off the chiles and shake the seeds out. In a small bowl, combine the 1 teaspoon cornstarch, 2 teaspoons water, soy, Sherry, honey and vinegar and set aside.
4. Heat the 3 tablespoons oil in a wok. Fry the chiles until they are almost black. Remove and drain on paper towels. Drain shrimp and fry about 30 seconds in the hot oil. Do not overcook. Add blended sauce, scallions, ginger and garlic and toss until sauce is smooth, about 1 minute. Return chiles to wok and toss again to combine. Serve over white rice.

PREPARATION AND COOKING TIME: 50 minutes
YIELD: 4 servings

Shrimp de Jonghe

A simple and quick recipe that also looks great.

1   *pound fresh shrimp, shelled and deveined*
8   *tablespoons butter*
1   *clove garlic, minced*
3   *tablespoons chopped parsley*
¼   *cup Sherry*
¼   *teaspoon dried tarragon*
¼   *teaspoon nutmeg*
¼   *teaspoon thyme*
¼   *teaspoon onion powder*
      salt and black pepper to taste
      Optional: ½ cup bread crumbs tossed with 2 tablespoons melted butter

1. Preheat oven to 400 degrees. Arrange shrimp in the bottom of a baking dish.
2. Melt the butter in a saucepan or skillet, add the garlic and cook for 2 minutes over medium heat. Stir in all remaining ingredients except the optional crumbs and pour over the shrimp. Top with optional crumbs if desired.
3. Bake uncovered in the preheated oven for about 15 minutes until shrimp turn pink and crumbs (if used) are browned. Serve over rice.

PREPARATION TIME: 15 minutes
COOKING TIME: 15 minutes
YIELD: 3-4 servings

Chimon Island is known for its heron rookery and has been making ornithological news since the birds began to breed there in the early 1960's. It is the only one of its kind in New England.

Crab-Stuffed Shrimp

This rich and delicious recipe also makes a great appetizer.

20   *jumbo shrimp, peeled and deveined*
½   *pound crabmeat*
1   *hard-cooked egg, finely chopped*
¼   *cup minced mushrooms*
1   *tablespoon chopped fresh dill*
½   *tablespoon chopped parsley*
½   *teaspoon Tabasco*
¼   *cup Sherry*
¼   *teaspoon dried basil*
¼   *teaspoon dried oregano*
      salt and black pepper to taste
⅓   *cup dry bread crumbs*
½   *cup whipping cream, or enough to moisten*
½   *cup (8 tablespoons) melted butter*
½   *cup Parmesan cheese*
      lemon wedges

1.   Preheat oven to 350 degrees.
2.   Split the shrimp open along the back to form a large pocket and place on a baking sheet.
3.   Combine remaining ingredients, except butter, cheese and lemon. Heap the stuffing generously into the shrimp, sprinkle with the melted butter and the Parmesan, and bake in the pre-heated oven for 15-25 minutes, depending on the size of the shrimp. Serve with lemon wedges.

PREPARATION TIME: 30-40 minutes
COOKING TIME: 20 minutes
YIELD: 4-6 as an entree
            8 as a first course

Westport Shrimp Curry

Substitute any firm-textured boneless fish. Monkfish, cut into 1½-inch pieces, would be ideal.

3   tablespoons butter
2   tablespoons oil
1½ cups chopped onion
1   rib celery, finely chopped
1   apple, such as MacIntosh, peeled and chopped
1   clove garlic, minced
1   teaspoon minced fresh ginger
1   tablespoon curry powder
1   tablespoon flour
2   cups water or shrimp stock (see note)
½   cup white wine
2-3 plum tomatoes, peeled, seeded and cut into thin strips
1¼ pounds shrimp, shelled and deveined
½   teaspoon salt or to taste
¼   teaspoon freshly ground black pepper
2-3 cups cooked rice
    mango chutney (purchased) as a condiment

1. Melt the butter and oil together in a large skillet. Add the onion and celery and cook over low heat, stirring occasionally, until onions are very soft but not browned, about 15 minutes. Add apple, garlic, and ginger and cook 3-5 minutes. Stir in curry powder and flour and cook, stirring over medium-high heat for 2 minutes. Gradually add water (or stock) and wine and bring to a simmer, stirring to incorporate. Add tomatoes and simmer uncovered for 10 minutes until sauce is slightly thickened.

2. Add shelled shrimp and cook for 3-4 minutes or until they turn pink. Season with salt and pepper. Serve over or around hot cooked rice and pass chutney as a condiment.

NOTE: To make shrimp stock, simmer rinsed shrimp shells in 2½ cups water for 20 minutes. Strain and use in the curry sauce for extra flavor.

PREPARATION TIME: 45 minutes
YIELD: 4 servings

Nancy's Scampi

10-14   *large shrimp*
¼   *pound (8 tablespoons) unsalted butter*
1½   *teaspoons minced garlic*
1   *teaspoon Worcestershire sauce*
2   *tablespoons parsley flakes*
1   *teaspoon paprika*
          Never Fail Rice (recipe follows)

1. Peel and devein shrimp. Melt the butter over low heat in a large skillet with a heat-proof handle (such as cast iron or copper). Stir in the garlic, Worcestershire and parsley flakes.
2. Preheat the broiler. Arrange the shrimp in a single layer in the butter and sprinkle liberally with the paprika. Cook over low heat for 3 minutes.
3. Place the skillet under the broiler approximately 5 inches from the heat source and cook until the shrimp look almost burned in places, about 5 minutes.
4. Arrange around rice on a heated platter or on individual plates.

PREPARATION AND COOKING TIME: 20 minutes
YIELD: 2 servings

Never Fail Rice

1¼ *cups water*
1   *small chicken bouillon cube*
½   *cup Uncle Ben's rice*

1. In a medium saucepan bring water and bouillon cube to the boil, breaking up bouillon cube with the side of a spoon. Add rice, return to boil, reduce heat and cook covered over very low heat for 25 minutes until liquid is absorbed.

PREPARATION AND COOKING TIME: 25 minutes
YIELD: 2 servings

Shrimp and Cheese Strata

This makes a wonderful brunch or luncheon dish. I serve it with an avocado and grapefruit salad with poppyseed dressing and crusty bread. Always gets rave reviews!

6   slices good-quality white bread
½   pound sharp cheddar cheese
1   pound cooked shrimp
¼   cup (4 tablespoons) unsalted butter, melted
3   eggs
½   teaspoon dry mustard
½   teaspoon salt, or to taste
2   cups milk

1. Break bread into pieces about the size of a quarter. Crumble or coarsely grate the cheese. In a buttered 2-quart casserole, layer the shrimp, bread cubes and cheese and pour melted butter over the top.
2. In a bowl, lightly beat the eggs with the mustard and salt. Stir in the milk. Pour egg-milk mixture over the mixture in the casserole. Cover with plastic wrap and refrigerate for at least 3 hours or for as long as overnight. (It really seems to benefit from the longer soaking time.)
3. Preheat oven to 350 degrees. Bake casserole uncovered for 20-30 minutes until puffed and browned. Serve immediately.

PREPARATION TIME: 30 minutes
COOKING TIME: 30 minutes
YIELD: 4 servings

Bali Prawns

This is a recipe from Indonesia.

2   *pounds shrimp, shelled and deveined*
     grated rind from 1 lemon
3   *tablespoons lemon juice*
½   *cup coconut milk (see instructions below)*
½   *teaspoon hot chili paste (available at Oriental markets)*
1   *tablespoon soy sauce*
1   *teaspoon brown sugar*
2   *cloves garlic, minced*
1   *teaspoon salt*
¼   *cup vegetable oil*

1. Make marinade by combining lemon rind and juice, coconut milk, chili paste, soy sauce, sugar, garlic and salt in a bowl. Mix until sugar is dissolved. Add shrimp, toss to coat evenly and marinate at least 15 minutes.
2. Prepare a barbecue fire. Thread 3 or 4 shrimp on bamboo skewers, brush with oil and grill over moderately hot coals until shrimp turn pink and begin to brown lightly, about 4 minutes.
3. Meanwhile, simmer remaining marinade for about 2 minutes, adding more coconut milk to taste. Serve as a dipping sauce for shrimp.

To Make Coconut Milk:

Put 2 cups grated coconut (can be packaged commercial variety) in a bowl and add 2½ cups very hot water. Let cool and strain through cheesecloth.

PREPARATION TIME: 30 minutes (excluding making coconut milk)
YIELD: 6-8 servings

Shrimp Dijon

2   *tablespoons butter*
24   *medium shrimp, peeled and deveined*
     salt
     about 6 turns of the peppermill
3½   *tablespoons finely chopped shallots*
1   *teaspoon paprika*
½   *teaspoon cayenne pepper*
⅓   *cup heavy cream*
2   *tablespoons Dijon mustard*
⅓   *cup sour cream*

1. Melt butter in a large skillet. Add shrimp, salt, pepper, shallots, paprika and cayenne pepper. Cook, stirring, over medium-high heat until shrimp turn pink, about 2 minutes. Add cream and mustard and simmer uncovered over medium heat until sauce has thickened somewhat, about 3-4 minutes.
2. Take pan off heat and stir in the sour cream. Return to stove and cook over low heat until heated through. Do not boil or sauce will curdle. Serve immediately over rice.

PREPARATION TIME: 20 minutes, including shelling shrimp
COOKING TIME: 10 minutes
YIELD: 4 servings

An adult oyster pumps as many as 100 gallons of water through its system daily. Clams and oysters are able to cleanse themselves and expel bacteria when placed in clean waters.

Le Mistral's Fillet of Red Snapper with Saffron Sauce

4   fillets of red snapper with skin left on
2   plum tomatoes
3   medium zucchini
2   tablespoons unsalted butter, divided
    a pinch of saffron threads
    juice of one lemon
1   shallot, minced
2   tablespoons heavy cream
    fresh ground white pepper
    salt
8   sprigs parsley

1. Wipe the snapper fillets with a damp paper towel and set aside.
2. Immerse the tomatoes in boiling water for 30 seconds, remove skin and cut in half and gently squeeze out seeds. Dice into small pieces.
3. Slice the zucchini on the diagonal into ovals. Place in a medium saucepan with ½ tablespoon of the butter and a pinch of salt and pepper. Cover with about 1½ cups cold water, bring to the boil, and cook for one minute. Remove zucchini with a slotted spoon to a plate, reserving the cooking liquid. Add a pinch of saffron threads to the zucchini liquid and set aside for 15 minutes.
4. Pour saffron-zucchini liquid into a large non-reactive skillet. Add another ½ tablespoon of butter, the lemon juice, and the chopped shallot. Bring to the boil and add the snapper fillets to the liquid, skin side up. Reduce heat, cover, and simmer for 2 minutes or until fish tests done. Remove fillets carefully with a large spatula and reserve on a plate.
5. Reduce the poaching liquid over medium-high heat to about ¾ cup. Add the cream and whisk in the remaining 1 tablespoon of

butter. Add the chopped tomato. Taste and season if necessary.

6. Preheat oven to 350 degrees. On four serving plates, place the fish, skin side up, and arrange the zucchini around the rim of the plates. Place plates in the preheated oven to heat for a couple of minutes. Spoon some sauce around the fish, without completely covering it. Garnish plates with sprigs of parsley and serve.

PREPARATION AND COOKING TIME: 40 minutes
YIELD: 4 servings

Sherried Shrimp

4   *tablespoons butter*
¼   *pound mushrooms, sliced*
1   *can frozen cream of shrimp soup, thawed*
1   *cup sour cream*
1   *teaspoon soy sauce*
¼   *teaspoon freshly ground pepper*
1½   *pounds cooked shrimp*
3   *tablespoons Sherry, or to taste*
1½   *cups raw rice, cooked*

1. Melt butter in a large skillet and sauté mushrooms over medium heat for 5 minutes. Add soup, sour cream, soy sauce and pepper and stir over low heat until smooth. Do not allow to boil or sour cream will curdle. Stir in shrimp and Sherry to taste and heat through.

2. Serve over rice.

PREPARATION AND COOKING TIME: 20 minutes
YIELD: 6 servings

Gullfish Snapper

Inspired by a recipe from cookbook author, Marcella Hazan.

1	(5-6 pound) whole golden or red snapper (see note)
16	mussels
8	fresh oysters, unshelled
8	large shrimp
2½	tablespoons chopped parsley
2	large or 4 small cloves garlic, crushed
½	cup plus 1 tablespoon good olive oil
	juice of 1 large lemon
6	tablespoons dry unflavored bread crumbs
3	tablespoons thinly sliced onion
1	tablespoon salt
	freshly ground pepper to taste
½-1	teaspoon dried oregano, optional

1. Preheat oven to 475 degrees.
2. Bone the fish accordingly: make a long slit on the underbelly of the fish from the head to the tail. Using a sharp knife, detach all rib bones from the upper half. Work your way in the same manner around the backbone and then the underside of the fish. Carefully separate this skeleton by snapping back the head and tail very gently. The entire structure will then detach in one piece leaving a boneless fish whose entire cavity can be stuffed.
3. Scrub and debeard the mussels under cold running water. Place in a saucepan along with about 1 tablespoon water. Cover and cook over high heat for a few minutes until the shells open. Remove the mussels from the pan with a slotted spoon, shuck and place them in a medium-size mixing bowl. Strain juices left in the pan through 2 thicknesses of paper towels and pour over the mussels.

4. Peel and devein shrimp and add to mussels. Shuck oysters and add along with any liquor to the mussels. Add remaining ingredients and toss to mix well.

5. Rinse the fish inside and out with cold water. Dry thoroughly with paper towels. In a long, shallow baking dish or pan, spread 2 thicknesses of heavy duty aluminum foil, enough to totally fold over and envelop the fish.

6. Place fish in pan and distribute the stuffing and juices in the interior cavity. Reserve some juice and rub it over the skin of the fish. Fold the foil over, making sure that the contents are tightly tucked in.

7. Bake 45-50 minutes. Allow to set for 5-10 minutes before serving. The fish will be very juicy and tender. Serve directly from the foil since the boneless fish can easily break and fall apart. Slice directly through the fish to serve.

NOTE: Boning the whole fish is a bit tricky. Many fishmongers will do this for you if you call in advance.

PREPARATION TIME: 1 hour
COOKING TIME: 50 minutes
YIELD: 4-6 servings

Braised Red Snapper Vera Cruz

Instead of red snapper, also try perch, catfish, or golden snapper. The recipe, created by Kelley G. Jones who is chef at the Sterling Ocean House in Stamford can easily be increased to serve more people.

2   *ounces (¼ cup) olive oil*
1   *(8-ounce) fillet red snapper*
     flour for dredging
4   *ounces (½ cup) white wine*
½   *small tomato, chopped*
½   *small onion, julienned*
1   *ounce capers, drained*
1   *small clove garlic, minced*
6-8 *pitted and sliced green olives*

1. In a 10″ sauté pan over high heat, heat the oil. Dredge the fish in flour, then place flesh-side down in the oil. Cook until lightly browned and then turn and cook on the second side, about 7-8 minutes total, or until fish tests done. Remove to a warm platter.
2. Pour off most of the oil in the pan. Add the white wine and cook, stirring up browned bits clinging to the bottom of the pan, for about 30 seconds. Add tomato, onion, capers, garlic, and olives. Reduce liquid by half.
3. Serve the fish with the sauce spooned over.

PREPARATION TIME: 8 minutes
COOKING TIME: 15 minutes
YIELD: 1 serving

★Grilled Red Snapper with Ginger and Sesame Oil

A fish dish with Oriental flavors.

1	*3-4 pound red snapper, cleaned and split*
¾	*inch piece of fresh ginger, peeled and minced*
1	*clove garlic, minced*
3	*shallots, minced*
½	*cup rice wine vinegar*
	juice of 1 lemon
3	*tablespoons soy sauce*
2	*tablespoons sesame oil*
¼	*cup sesame seeds, toasted (see note)*

1. Wipe inside and outside of fish dry with paper towels. Combine all ingredients except sesame seeds in a glass dish and marinate the fish in the refrigerator for at least 2 hours or for as long as overnight.
2. Preheat broiler or prepare a barbecue fire. Grease rack.
3. Remove fish from marinade, place on broiling pan or directly on grill and cook about 4 minutes per side, or until fish tests done, basting occasionally with the marinade.
4. Sprinkle with sesame seeds before serving.

NOTE: To toast sesame seeds, place in a heavy skillet and cook over medium heat, stirring frequently, for about 5 minutes, or until golden and fragrant. Transfer to a bowl or plastic container to cool.

PREPARATION TIME: 20 minutes (excluding marinating time)
COOKING TIME: 9-10 minutes
YIELD: 4 servings

Sole with Lemon and Capers

Our testers both found this recipe to be exceptionally easy and elegant.

4   *sole fillets—about 6 ounces each (lemon sole is excellent)*
½   *cup milk*
½   *cup vegetable oil*
¼   *cup (4 tablespoons) unsalted butter*
½   *cup flour*
1   *large lemon, peeled, seeded, and cut into ¼ inch cubes*
3   *tablespoons drained capers*
1   *tablespoon chopped parsley*

1.   Soak the sole fillets in the milk for about 30 minutes.
2.   Heat the oil and 1 tablespoon of the butter in a large skillet. Remove fish from milk, dredge in the flour and cook in the skillet over medium-high heat until lightly browned, about 2 minutes per side. Remove fish to a serving platter.
3.   Discard the cooking oil and wipe the skillet out with paper towels. Add the remaining 3 tablespoons butter to the skillet and cook over medium heat until butter foams up a little and turns a light brown. Remove from heat, stir in the chopped lemon, capers and parsley, and pour sauce over the sole fillets.

PREPARATION TIME: 30 minutes (including soaking fish)
COOKING TIME: 10 minutes
YIELD: 4 servings

Connecticut leads the country as the most intensely shellfished area per acre of shoreline. The Bureau of Fisheries reports that over 2,600 metric tons of seafood come from these waters annually.

Fillet of Sole with Rosemary and Basil

One of our testers commented that this dish is easy, pretty—and low in calories!

1½   tablespoons safflower oil
3   shallots, chopped
4   thin sole or flounder fillets
3   tablespoons fresh basil, chopped
½   teaspoon rosemary
      freshly ground black pepper to taste
4   tablespoons white wine
3   tablespoons lemon juice
2   tablespoons chopped fresh sorrel (or parsley) for garnish

1. Preheat oven to 350 degrees. Lightly butter a 9 x 12" baking dish and sprinkle shallots over the bottom.
2. Sprinkle fish with the herbs and pepper. Starting with the short end, loosely roll each fillet into a cylinder and place the rolls seam side down in the baking dish. Pour wine and lemon juice over the fish and bake in the preheated oven for about 20 minutes, basting occasionally with the liquid. Remove from the oven and sprinkle with the chopped sorrel or parsley before serving.

PREPARATION TIME: 15 minutes
COOKING TIME: 20 minutes
YIELD: 4 servings

The importance of fish to the economy of the colonies is reflected in the fact that the first public school in America was paid for with the taxes from cod and mackerel fishing.

★Fillet of Sole Supreme

Delicious served with parslied rice.

1   cup cream
1½   cups milk
¼   cup (4 tablespoons) unsalted butter
½   small onion, finely chopped
¼   cup flour
       salt and pepper to taste
¼   cup (4 tablespoons) unsalted butter for mushrooms
½   pound mushrooms, cleaned and sliced
1   teaspoon lemon juice
2   pounds fillet of sole or other firm white fish (about 12 fillets)
       Lawry's seasoning salt
3   tomatoes, thinly sliced
12   thin slices Swiss cheese (6-8 ounces)

1. To make the Bechamel sauce, bring the cream and milk to the boil in a small saucepan and set aside. In a heavy medium saucepan, melt the butter, add the onion and sauté over low heat for 5 minutes, until softened. Stir in the flour and cook over medium heat for 2 minutes. Gradually whisk in the scalded cream and milk and whisk until smooth. Simmer over very low heat, stirring occasionally, for 5-10 minutes. Season to taste with salt and pepper.
2. In a skillet, melt the butter and sauté the mushrooms over medium heat for about 5 minutes, until they are beginning to brown. Sprinkle with the lemon juice and add the mushrooms to the Bechamel. Set aside.
3. Sprinkle both sides of the fish fillets with the Lawry's seasoning salt. Roll up each fillet and place seam side down in a buttered 9 x 13″ baking dish. Place one slice of tomato and one slice of cheese

between each fish roll. Pour sauce over fish. Casserole may be made ahead to this point.

4. Preheat oven to 350 degrees. Bake casserole uncovered for 20 minutes or until fish tests done and sauce is bubbly.

PREPARATION TIME: 40 minutes
COOKING TIME: 20 minutes
YIELD: 5-6 servings

Puffy Broiled Sole

The coating on this really does puff up nicely under the broiler.

4   *fillets of sole (approximately 1 pound total)*
1   *small onion, thinly sliced*
1   *cup mayonnaise*
4   *tablespoons grated Parmesan cheese*
    lemon wedges

1. Preheat the broiler. Rinse fillets and pat dry. Arrange in a single layer in a glass or stainless steel broiler-safe baking dish.
2. Separate onion into rings and arrange over fillets. Combine mayonnaise and cheese and spread over the fish. Cover dish with foil, making sure foil does not touch the fish.
3. Broil, covered, for 10-15 minutes, or until fish is almost done. Remove foil and broil until topping is puffed and browned and bubbly, 2-3 minutes. Serve with wedges of lemon.

PREPARATION TIME: 10 minutes
COOKING TIME: 13-16 minutes
YIELD: 3-4 servings

Fillet of Sole with Anchovies

If the anchovy garnish isn't to your taste, try lemon wedges and parsley sprigs.

2   *pounds fillet of sole*
     salt and freshly ground black pepper to taste
     flour
¼   *cup olive oil*
2   *tablespoons mashed anchovy fillets or 1 tablespoon anchovy*
        paste
1   *stick (8 tablespoons) unsalted butter, melted*
6   *whole anchovy fillets, optional*
     lemon wedges and parsley sprigs, optional

1. Cut the sole into 6 servings. Sprinkle lightly with salt and pep-
    per. Dredge in a small amount of flour and shake off excess.
2. Heat oil in a large skillet and fry fish, over medium heat and
    turning once, for 6-8 minutes until browned on both sides and
    cooked through. Transfer to a warm platter.
3. Combine the mashed anchovies and melted butter and pour over
    fish. Garnish with whole anchovies or lemon and parsley.

PREPARATION TIME: 20 minutes
YIELD: 6 servings

★Simply Savory Baked Fish

This recipe was given to our contributor's family in 1955 by a woman friend who was an advertising executive—a rarity in those days! She must have liked the fact that this dish is not only delicious, but *extremely* easy and quick to prepare.

1 ½ *pounds white fish fillets (sole, flounder, haddock, scrod), rinsed*
       and patted dry
1   *cup bread crumbs, preferably homemade*

½ cup (8 tablespoons) butter
1 tablespoon cider vinegar
1 tablespoon Worcestershire sauce
1 tablespoon lemon juice
1 teaspoon prepared mustard (or more to taste)

1. Preheat the oven to 350 degrees. Place the bread crumbs on a
    shallow plate, dredge the fish in the crumbs, and arrange the fil-
    lets in a single layer in an 8 x 14″ baking dish.
2. In a small saucepan, melt the butter with the vinegar, Worces-
    tershire, lemon juice and mustard, and pour the sauce evenly
    over the fish. Bake uncovered in the preheated oven for 20 min-
    utes, basting every 5 minutes or so. Serve directly from the bak-
    ing dish.

PREPARATION TIME: 10 minutes
COOKING TIME: 20 minutes
YIELD: 4 servings

Catch of the Day Fillets

A wonderful family dinner and very pretty sprinkled with a little chopped
parsley and garnished with lemon wedges.

6 fillets of white fish such as sole or flounder
⅓ cup vegetable oil
2 cups crushed corn flakes

1. Preheat oven to 450 degrees.
2. Pat the fillets dry and cut each into quarters. Dip the fillets into
    the oil and then into the corn flakes. Shake off excess corn flakes.
3. Place the fish on a baking sheet and bake for 10 minutes until
    crispy and fish is cooked through.

PREPARATION TIME: 5 minutes
BAKING TIME: 10 minutes
YIELD: 6 servings

★Grilled Red Snapper

This is adapted from a recipe that appeared in the *Hay Day Newsletter* in
the summer of 1985.

4   *fillets of red snapper (about 6 ounces each)*
1   *tablespoon olive oil*
      salt and black pepper

Sauce

1   *tablespoon unsalted butter*
1   *tablespoon flour*
¼   *cup bottled clam juice*
¼   *cup dry white wine*
½   *cup heavy cream*
2   *tablespoons chopped fresh dill or 1 teaspoon dried*
½   *teaspoon salt, or to taste*
⅛   *teaspoon black pepper, or to taste*
1   *teaspoon additional unsalted butter*
      paprika

1. Prepare a barbecue fire or preheat the broiler.
2. Brush the fish fillets with the olive oil and sprinkle lightly with
    salt and pepper. When fire is ready place the fish directly on an
    oiled grill or use a hinged grill basket. Or fish may be cooked in
    the oven broiler. Cook 2-3 minutes per side or until fish tests
    done. Place on a serving platter and keep warm.
3. To make the sauce, melt the tablespoon of butter in a saucepan,
    stir in the flour and cook, stirring, for 3 minutes over medium
    heat. Do not brown. Add clam juice and wine and whisk over
    medium heat for one minute until thick and smooth. Stir in
    cream, dill, salt and pepper and heat through. Remove from heat

and beat in the final teaspoon of butter for enrichment. Pour sauce over fish and sprinkle with paprika. Serve with buttered pasta and a salad of light lettuces.

PREPARATION AND COOKING TIME: 30 minutes
YIELD: 4 servings

Banana Sole

This recipe comes from South America.

4	*fillets of lemon sole*
4	*tablespoons butter*
¼	*teaspoon lemon pepper*
1	*egg, lightly beaten*
1	*cup bread crumbs*
4	*bananas, ripe but firm*
3	*tablespoons butter*

1. Preheat the broiler.
2. Melt the 4 tablespoons of butter with the lemon pepper. In a shallow dish, combine the butter with the beaten egg. Place the bread crumbs in another shallow dish.
3. Dip the sole fillets in the butter-egg mixture and then roll in the crumbs. Arrange on a broiler pan and cook 4-5 inches from the heat source for 3-4 minutes per side, or until browned on the outside and fish tests done.
4. Meanwhile, peel bananas and cut in half lengthwise. Melt the 3 tablespoons butter in a large skillet. Cook banana halves over medium-high heat for about 4 minutes until caramelized. Serve each piece of sole topped with two banana slices.

PREPARATION AND COOKING TIME: 20 minutes
YIELD: 4 servings

Rolled Sole Fairfield

Both testers liked this recipe *very* much and appreciated the fact that it
was quick and easy to make.

6   *fillets of sole (1-1¹/₂ pounds)*
2   *cups crushed Ritz crackers*
¹/₃   *cup melted butter*
¹/₃   *cup white wine*
1   *teaspoon lemon juice*
1   *teaspoon chopped parsley*
¹/₈   *teaspoon garlic powder*
        paprika
6   *thin slices of lemon*

1.   Preheat oven to 350 degrees. Rinse and pat dry fish fillets.
2.   In a mixing bowl combine cracker crumbs, melted butter, wine,
      lemon juice, parsley and garlic powder. Divide crumb mixture
      equally among the six fillets, spreading it evenly over the fish.
      Roll up fillets and place seam-side down in a lightly greased
      shallow baking dish. Sprinkle lightly with paprika, place a lemon
      slice on each rolled fillet and bake in preheated oven for 20 min-
      utes, basting with any accumulated juices once or twice.

PREPARATION TIME: 15 minutes
COOKING TIME: 20 minutes
YIELD: 4 servings

*Greenfield Hill in Fairfield is one of the most beautiful as well as historic
sections of the county. Many of its stately homes were built in the late 18th
century as it was a favored spot where privateers and sea captains chose
to retire.*

★Lemony Stuffed Sole Fillets

6   *tablespoons butter*
⅓   *cup chopped celery*
2   *tablespoons chopped shallots or onions*
1   *cup herb-seasoned stuffing mix*
1   *tablespoon chopped parsley*
1   *tablespoon lemon juice*
¼   *teaspoon salt*
¼   *teaspoon pepper*
4   *large thin fish fillets such as sole or flounder (1-1½ pounds total)*
4   *tablespoons butter*
1   *teaspoon dried dill*

1. Preheat oven to 350 degrees.
2. Melt the 6 tablespoons butter in a skillet and sauté the celery and chopped onion for 2 minutes. Add stuffing mix, parsley and lemon juice and toss gently to combine. Season with salt and pepper to taste.
3. Cut each fish fillet in half to make eight 3" x 4" pieces. Place four of the pieces in a 9-inch square baking pan. Top each piece of fish with some of the stuffing and then cover each with the remaining halves of the fillets.
4. Melt 4 tablespoons butter in a small saucepan and stir in the dill. Pour dill butter over the fillets and bake in the preheated oven for about 20 minutes or until fish tests almost done. Spoon accumulated buttery juices over the top of the fish, return to the oven and bake for 5 minutes more.

PREPARATION TIME: 30 minutes
COOKING TIME: 25 minutes
YIELD: 4 servings

A.E. Hotchner's Spanish Swordfish

2   *pounds swordfish steak, cut 2 inches thick*
1   *cup Newman's Own Salad Dressing*
¼   *cup lime juice*
1   *tablespoon thyme or rosemary*
    lemon juice
    butter
    pine boughs

1. Marinate swordfish in Newman's Own Salad Dressing, lime juice and thyme or rosemary for several hours.
2. Prepare charcoal and, when coals are gray, place fish on the grill. Saturate with lemon juice and chunks of butter and cook 10 minutes on each side, turning only once and putting more lemon juice, butter and marinade on the turned side. Remove fish, place a freshly cut pine bough on the fire, put the fish on top of the pine bough, and let it be seared by the flame. Remove immediately after the pine flame dies down and serve.

PREPARATION TIME: 20 minutes (excluding marinating time)
COOKING TIME: 25 minutes
YIELD: 4-6 servings

Daniel Sherwood built the first house on Sherwood Island where he raised ten children. In a short time they took over the entire island in name as well as possession. His three youngest sons were triplets—Francis, Franklin, and Frederick. Born in 1810, they all eventually became sea captains, and each owned his own vessel. They often met in the same port, trading between New York and southern coastal towns. They looked so much alike that they often played jokes on unsuspecting folk. They were hale and hearty men who were of sterling Yankee character.

Mustard Swordfish

The contributor made this up—a result of experimenting with her mustard collection. She likes it with fresh asparagus and a tossed salad.

2   *pounds swordfish steaks, 1¹/₂ inches thick*
³/₄   *cup mayonnaise*
¹/₄   *cup stone ground or coarse-grain mustard*
1   *tablespoon dry white wine*
1   *tablespoon lemon juice*
1   *scallion, sliced thinly*

1.   Prepare a barbecue fire or preheat the oven broiler.
2.   Rinse and pat the swordfish dry. Combine remaining ingredients and spread on both sides of the fish.
3.   Grill over white coals or in the oven broiler, turning once, until fish is firm, about 15-20 minutes total. Serve with any remaining marinade and lemon wedges.

PREPARATION TIME: 15 minutes
COOKING TIME: 15 minutes
YIELD: 4-6 servings

Connecticut's jagged coastline dotted with coves and inlets was well-suited to the exploits of pirates, including the notorious Captain Kidd. Kidd supposedly made several visits to Sachem's Head in Guilford and what is now Captain Kidd's Punchbowl in the Thimble Islands. Although locals have their favorite tales of buried treasure, no one has ever really substantiated the stories.

Fern's Swordfish Provençale en Papillote

This comes from Fern's Restaurant in New Milford, CT. The recipe is written for a single serving, but can easily be expanded to any number.

1   *large sheet parchment paper*
1   *tablespoon vegetable oil*
1   *swordfish steak (6-8 ounces)*
2   *fresh plum tomatoes, diced*
½   *clove garlic, crushed*
    salt and pepper to taste
2   *tablespoons white wine*
    juice of ¹/₂ lemon

1.   Cut parchment paper in a large heart shape.
2.   Heat the oil in a skillet and brown the swordfish for about one minute over high heat. Remove fish from pan. Add the tomatoes and garlic and sauté over medium-low heat for about 3 minutes. Season with salt, pepper and white wine.
3.   Place the swordfish on right hand side of parchment paper. Squeeze lemon juice over fish and top with tomato mixture. Fold parchment paper in half and then fold, starting at the top and make small folds all around the edge. Tuck last fold underneath to seal.
4.   Preheat oven to 350 degrees.
5.   Place the fish on a baking sheet and bake 15-20 minutes until puffed, parchment is lightly browned and fish is cooked through. Serve straight from the oven by slitting open the parchment hearts.

PREPARATION TIME: 10 minutes
BAKING TIME: 15-20 minutes
YIELD: 1 serving

Grilled Skewered Swordfish with Mustard Marinade

Swordfish cut in large chunks like this takes particularly well to grilling, but the fish can also be cooked in the stove broiler. Serve with asparagus, buttered pasta and a bottle of lovely white wine on a summer evening.

1½-1¾	*pounds swordfish*
1	*cup olive oil*
¼	*cup Dijon mustard*
¼	*cup lemon juice*
3	*tablespoons minced shallots*
2	*large cloves garlic, minced*
1	*tablespoon chopped fresh dill or 1 teaspoon dried dill*
1	*teaspoon salt*
½	*teaspoon pepper*

1. Cut swordfish into 2-inch chunks. In a mixing bowl combine oil, mustard, lemon juice, shallots, garlic, dill, salt and pepper. Add fish and stir gently so that it is entirely coated with marinade. Marinate for at least three hours or as long as overnight.
2. Prepare a charcoal fire or preheat a gas grill or the oven broiler. Thread swordfish on four 12-inch skewers and grill or broil for 10-15 minutes, turning frequently and basting with reserved marinade until fish tests done. Place skewers on serving platter or on individual plates, drizzle with any remaining marinade and serve.

PREPARATION TIME: 20 minutes (excluding marinating time)
COOKING TIME: 15 minutes
YIELD: 4 servings

Tuna Steaks Niçoise

4   *tuna steaks, approximately 1 inch thick (about 1¹/₂ pounds total)*
2   *tablespoons olive oil*
¹/₂   *teaspoon dried thyme*
      freshly ground pepper to taste
2   *tablespoons finely chopped scallions*
1   *tablespoon finely chopped green olives*
1   *tablespoon chopped capers*
1   *teaspoon finely chopped green peppercorns*
2   *tablespoons Balsamic vinegar*
1   *teaspoon anchovy paste*
¹/₂   *cup olive oil*
2   *tablespoons finely chopped parsley*
1   *tablespoon Pernod*

1. Place tuna steaks in a large bowl, add the oil, thyme and pepper and turn to coat well.
2. To make the sauce, combine the scallions, olives, capers, peppercorns and vinegar in a small bowl. Beat in the anchovy paste and the oil. Stir in parsley and Pernod. Sauce may be made ahead and stored for several hours in the refrigerator. Bring back to room temperature before using.
3. Lightly oil and heat a skillet large enough to hold the tuna steaks in one layer. When skillet is hot, place fish in the pan and cook for 3 minutes per side, or until it reaches desired degree of doneness. (Tuna should be cooked slightly rare or it tends to be dry.)
4. Transfer fish to a warm platter, spoon half of the sauce over the fish and pass remaining sauce at the table.

PREPARATION AND COOKING TIME: 45 minutes
YIELD: 4 servings

Easy Chinese Tuna Casserole

2   cans tuna, drained
1   can cream of mushroom soup
¼   cup water
2   teaspoons soy sauce
1   cup cashews, unsalted if available (if salted are used, rinse and
     drain on paper towels)
1   4-ounce can mushrooms
½   cup chopped green onions
1   cup chopped celery
2   cups chow mein noodles

1. Preheat oven to 375 degrees. Combine all but 1 cup of the noo-
    dles in a large bowl and mix well. Turn into a greased 2-quart
    casserole and sprinkle remaining noodles on top.
2. Bake uncovered in preheated oven for 30-40 minutes until
    heated through.

PREPARATION TIME: 10 minutes
COOKING TIME: 30-40 minutes
YIELD: 6 servings

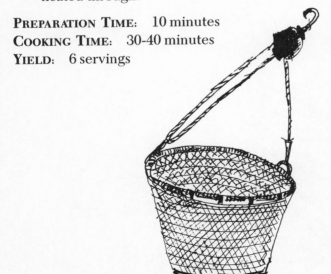

Grilled Tuna with Ginger

4   *individual tuna steaks cut 1 inch thick or 1 large steak*
     salt and pepper to taste
1   *tablespoon grated fresh ginger*
1   *tablespoon lemon juice*
1   *tablespoon olive oil*

1.   Preheat broiler or outdoor grill.
2.   Rub both sides of tuna with salt and pepper, ginger, lemon juice and oil. Cover and let stand at room temperature until ready to cook.
3.   Broil or grill for 2-3 minutes per side for medium rare tuna. If broiling, place fish 6 inches from heat source and leave door partially open. If grilling, place on hot grill and cover grill while cooking.
4.   Serve with Sauce Provençale, page 104, if desired.

PREPARATION TIME: 10 minutes
COOKING TIME: 5-6 minutes
YIELD: 4 servings

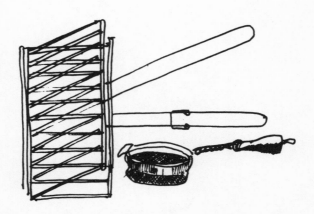

Mill Pond Broiled Trout

This recipe may be adjusted according to the number of people you are serving. Have your fishmonger fillet the trout for you.

2   *trout fillets per person*
For Each Fillet:
  a sprinkle of garlic salt
  a sprinkle of pepper
  a pinch of dried dill
  a sprinkle of Worcestershire sauce
  about 2 teaspoons Italian-style bread crumbs
  2 teaspoons butter
  lemon wedges for garnish

1. Preheat the broiler.
2. Arrange trout fillets on a broiler pan and sprinkle each with garlic salt, pepper, dill, Worcestershire and bread crumbs. Dot with butter.
3. Broil 4 inches from heat source for approximately 5 minutes until fish tests done and crumbs are brown. Serve with lemon wedges.

PREPARATION TIME: 5 minutes
COOKING TIME: 5 minutes
YIELD: Dependent upon number of fillets cooked

The only extensive scalloping today in Connecticut is in the Niantic River. Eel grass is important in the reproductive cycle of scallops as the junior scallops attach themselves to the grass so they aren't swept away by the current.

Darien, Stamford, &
Greenwich

If you overhear people in this neck of the woods jawing about winds, tides, currents and navigation, chances are they could be any "old salt" of the sea. If their discussion turns to rigging, tactics and strategy, you might want to listen for "tips" because the subject is probably about racing. Stick around long enough and you'll not only get a glimpse of a regatta first hand but will most likely get caught up in the spirit as well, for this is yachting territory. These folks have been at it for a long time, as citizens of their towns' established yacht clubs well before the turn of the century.

The 1890's ushered in the Golden Decade of Yachting, an era of elegant attire, correct nautical manners and professional crews who spit-and-polished owners' vessels. Summer colonies and seaside resorts flourished as a result of this leisured monied class whose beautiful cottages and estates dotted the shoreline and rolling landscapes. Although Stamford in these days was already an urban industrial town, Darien and Greenwich maintained a more rural flavor with a landed gentry that commuted by railroad or sloop to Wall Street. Luckily, one did not have to be rich to enjoy all of the pleasures of the sea as swimming became a popular pastime for all classes. Impressionist painters captured and immortalized these scenes on canvas, with the harbors and coastline of these parts favorite subjects and backdrops of the Cos Cob School. It was an era that lasted through the First World War.

Today, Stamford is still an urban center whose base of Fortune 500 companies ranks sixth in the country. Although Darien and Greenwich have their share of corporate headquarters, there is an atmosphere in these communities of tree-lined streets and stately homes which suggests the good life. Those who work hard often play hard, however and yachting continues to be a favorite sport and recreation.

SALADS

Times may have changed since the Victorian era, and slickers and deck shoes may have replaced the elegant attire of earlier days. Nonetheless, yachting is reminiscent of a sport that is rich and alive with color and tradition. It is hard to not be moved by things nautical. Whether it be the excitment of the thundering cannon that welcomes each finishing yacht in the Stamford-Vineyard race, the beauty and grace of sails and sleek craft gliding across windy waters, the nostalgia of old charts and maps lining yacht club walls, or the precision and well-ordered moves of a synchronized crew.... These are the things which move our spirit and speak to the sailor in all of us.

Pasta Salad with Marinated Oysters

This recipe is adapted from the *Maryland Seafood Cookbook*.

1	*pint oysters*
1	*cup (approximately) Italian salad dressing*
1	*cup cooked spiral pasta*
1	*cup cooked spinach noodles*
1	*cup cooked elbow macaroni*
½	*cup celery, sliced diagonally*
½	*cup carrots, sliced into ¼-inch rounds*
½	*cup radishes, sliced thinly*
½	*cup green or sweet red pepper, sliced*
½	*cup broccoli florettes*
¼	*cup chopped parsley*

1. The night before serving the salad, poach oysters in their own liquor and enough water to cover until their edges begin to ruffle, about 4 minutes. Drain and marinate in about ½ cup of the salad dressing overnight.

2. Cook pastas according to package directions; drain and rinse in cold water until pasta is cold. Prepare vegetables. Combine pastas, vegetables and drained oysters; toss gently to mix, adding additional dressing as needed. Cover and refrigerate for at least one hour. Serve on a lettuce bed with extra dressing on the side.

PREPARATION AND COOKING TIME: 1 hour
YIELD: 6-8 servings

The Five Mile River which borders Darien and Rowayton is actually only one mile long.

Cold Seafood Rice Salad

This makes a nice luncheon or supper dish and is also good made with cold chicken or other leftover meat.

3   *cups cooked rice*
2   *cups cooked shrimp or lobster*
½   *pound raw mushrooms, wiped clean and thinly sliced*
1   *cup water chestnuts, drained and sliced*
1   *cup chopped green pepper*
3   *pimientos, thinly sliced, or one 4-ounce jar sliced roasted*
    peppers
¼   *cup chopped parsley*
¼   *cup chopped chives*
    salt and black pepper to taste

Dressing:

3   *tablespoons vinegar*
3   *tablespoons soy sauce*
2   *teaspoons Dijon mustard*
1   *cup olive oil*
½   *teaspoon Tabasco*

1. In a large mixing bowl combine the rice, seafood, mushrooms, water chestnuts, green pepper, pimientos, parsley and chives.
2. Mix the dressing in a small bowl, pour it over the rice mixture and toss salad gently with a fork to combine. Taste and add salt and pepper as desired. Cover and refrigerate for at least one hour to allow flavors to mellow.

PREPARATION TIME: 45 minutes
YIELD: 6-7 servings

Shrimp and Endive Salad

This lovely composed salad makes an elegant luncheon dish. Or, arrange individual portions as a first course for a dinner party.

Herbed Mayonnaise:

½   *cup Hellmann's mayonnaise*
⅓   *cup sour cream*
2   *tablespoons chopped parsley*
2   *tablespoons minced chives*
2   *tablespoons minced fresh tarragon or 1 tablespoon dried*
2   *hard-cooked eggs, chopped*
2   *teaspoons fresh lemon juice*
2   *teaspoons white wine vinegar*
1   *teaspoon Dijon mustard*
     salt and freshly ground pepper to taste

Salad Ingredients:

7-8 *cups water*
2   *tablespoons salt*
2½   *pounds medium or large shrimp, unpeeled*
½   *head Romaine lettuce*
1   *head radicchio*
½   *head Belgian endive*
1   *8-ounce can water chestnuts, drained and sliced*
1   *medium green pepper, cut into julienne strips.*
6   *radishes, thinly sliced*
2   *medium tomatoes, cut in wedges*
4   *tablespoons alfalfa sprouts*

1. To make the Herbed Mayonnaise, combine all ingredients and mix well. Cover and refrigerate for at least 5 hours.
2. For the salad, bring salted water to a boil in a large pot. Add the shrimp and cook for 3 minutes. Drain and rinse with cold water and drain again. Chill for at least one hour.
3. Peel and devein the shrimp.
4. Arrange Romaine and radicchio leaves on a large serving platter or on individual plates. Arrange endive spears, shrimp, water chestnuts, green pepper, radishes, tomatoes and alfalfa sprouts on top. Top with a spoonful of Herbed Mayonnaise or pass the mayonnaise at the table.

PREPARATION AND COOKING TIME: 1 hour
YIELD: 6 servings

Crab-Stuffed Tomatoes

Makes great use of Connecticut's summer crop of tomatoes.

2   *cups garden lettuce, shredded*
2   *large ripe tomatoes from your garden*
6   *ounces crabmeat, frozen or fresh*
2   *scallions, chopped*
1   *rib celery, chopped*
1   *cup Miracle Whip*
    fresh cracked pepper to taste

1. Divide lettuce on two salad plates. Quarter tomatoes and arrange on top of lettuce in an attractive spoke pattern.
2. Combine remaining ingredients in a bowl and toss. Top tomatoes with the crab mixture and serve.

PREPARATION TIME: 20 minutes
YIELD: 2 servings

★Shrimp Salad with Snow Peas and Water Chestnuts

½   *pound snow peas, strings removed*
¾   *pound cooked shrimp*
1   *cup sliced canned water chestnuts, drained*
2   *tablespoons light soy sauce*
1   *tablespoon rice vinegar*
2   *tablespoons honey*
     juice of 1 lemon
½   *cup light vegetable oil*

1.   Bring a large pot of water to the boil. Blanch the snow peas in rapidly boiling water for 30 seconds. Drain and refresh under cold water. Drain again.
2.   Arrange the shrimp, snow peas and water chestnuts in a serving dish. Combine all remaining ingredients for the dressing and pour it over the salad. Toss well and serve.

PREPARATION AND COOKING TIME: 30 minutes
YIELD: 4-6 servings for lunch

Commodore Elias C. Benedict, a prominent leader in Greenwich, was known to host the rich and famous aboard his yacht, the Oneida. *It is surmised that he concocted "Eggs Benedict" while entertaining President Grover Cleveland during the summer of 1893. That same summer, the President had a successful surgical operation aboard the yacht, a fact that was concealed from the American public.*

Paella Salad

The flavors of paella in salad form.

1   (7-ounce) package yellow rice
4   tablespoons tarragon vinegar
⅓   cup oil
⅛   teaspoon salt
⅛   teaspoon dry mustard
2   cups diced cooked chicken
½   pound cooked shrimp
1   large green pepper, seeded and chopped
⅓   cup minced onion
½   cup thinly sliced celery
3   tablespoons chopped pimiento
    sliced tomatoes and cucumbers for garnish if desired

1. Cook rice according to package directions.
2. In a small bowl whisk together the vinegar, oil, salt and mus-
    tard. Turn rice into a mixing bowl, pour dressing over it and set
    aside to cool.
3. Cut shrimp in half and add chicken, shrimp and all remaining
    ingredients except the optional garnish to the rice. Toss well to
    combine. Refrigerate until ready to serve. Transfer to a bowl or
    shallow platter and garnish with tomatoes and cucumbers if
    desired.

PREPARATION AND COOKING TIME: 45 minutes
YIELD: 6 servings

*The Stamford-Denmark Friendship Race is an annual regatta which has
taken place since 1966. The race is part of a weeklong series of events in a
program to develop and promote trade and tourism between Stamford and
Denmark.*

★Salade Nicoise

While the recipe originated with Julia Child, it has been changed considerably.

3	cups cold blanched green beans
3 or 4	large tomatoes, quartered
3	cups cold blanched sliced zucchini or yellow squash
1	cup French vinaigrette (recipe follows)
1	head Boston lettuce, leaves separated
3	cups cold French potato salad (recipe follows)
1	cup canned tuna chunks, drained
½	cup pitted black olives, preferably the French kind
2 or 3	hardboiled eggs, peeled and quartered
6 to 12	drained anchovy fillets
2	tablespoons minced parsley
2	tablespoons other fresh herbs, minced, such as basil or tarragon

1. Combine the beans, tomatoes and squash in a bowl and toss with about ¼ cup of the vinaigrette. Line a large glass bowl or deep platter with the lettuce leaves and drizzle with about a tablespoon of the dressing. Then arrange the ingredients in the following order attractively in layers on top of the lettuce: first the bean/tomato mixture, then the potato salad, the tuna, the olives, eggs, and anchovies. Pour remaining dressing over all and sprinkle the herbs on top of the salad. Salad may be put together up to 2 hours ahead of time and kept covered in the refrigerator.
2. Show it to whomever you are serving it to because it looks very pretty. Toss and serve.

The Byram River in Greenwich got its name from early rum-running expeditions—"Buy Rum".

French Vinaigrette:

½   cup wine vinegar (Balsamic is especially good)
½   teaspoon dry mustard
2   garlic cloves, split
1½   cups good green olive oil
        fresh pepper and salt to taste

1. Combine vinegar, mustard and garlic in a small bowl. Gradually whisk in the oil. Season to taste with salt and pepper. Remove garlic clove before serving. This recipe yields enough to dress the potato salad as well as the Salad Nicoise, with some left over.

French Potato Salad:

4-5   medium potatoes, boiled until tender, peeled and sliced
2   tablespoons dry white wine
2   tablespoons minced chives
⅓   cup French vinaigrette

1. Toss the potatoes while still warm with the wine and set aside to cool. Toss with chives and the vinaigrette. Cover and refrigerate for at least one hour.

PREPARATION AND COOKING TIME: 1½ hours
YIELD: 6-8 servings

The Bush-Holley House in Cos Cob is not only the home of the Greenwich Historical Society since 1957 but is steeped in history of its own. It was once the home of David Bush, the wealthiest man in Greenwich. As a point of trade for packet boats leaving for New York, it eventually became the center for all mercantile trade in the area. When the house was sold in 1848 to George Smith, it became a boarding house until it was sold again to Edward Holley in 1882. As a vacation place, the "Holley Inn" attracted New York Impressionist painter John Twatchman whose presence attracted other famous painters and writers including Childe Hassam, Lincoln Steffens, and Willa Cather. The house remained an art colony until after World War I. Today, the visitor can see the furnishings and evidence of the times of all three families.

Seafood and Rice Salad

This lovely summer seafood salad could be made in quantity for a buffet.

1	*pound bay scallops or shrimp*
3	*thin slices onion*
2	*sprigs parsley*
2	*sprigs thyme*
1½	*cups white wine, or more if needed*
¾	*cup bottled or homemade Italian dressing, or more as needed*
1	*cup raw long grain rice*
	salt to taste
	cayenne pepper to taste
	Romaine lettuce leaves for lining serving platter
	sliced cucumber for garnish
	sliced-red onion for garnish
2	*teaspoons capers, drained*

1. In a wide saucepan poach the scallops with the onion, parsley, thyme, and enough white wine to cover. Cook gently for 2-3 minutes until scallops have turned opaque. Drain and reserve the poaching liquid for cooking the rice. Marinate the scallops in about ¼ cup of the dressing for at least an hour.
2. Measure the reserved poaching liquid and add enough water to make 2 cups. Bring the liquid to a boil in a saucepan, add the rice, and cook, covered, on lowest heat, for 25 minutes or until rice is tender. Turn rice into a bowl, fluff with a fork, and allow to cool for a few minutes.
3. Add scallops to the rice, toss with enough of the remaining dressing to moisten and season with salt and cayenne pepper. Cover and refrigerate.
4. Line a serving platter with a bed of Romaine leaves and pour the salad onto the lettuce. Decorate with sliced cucumber and thin rings of onion and sprinkle with capers before serving. Pass additional dressing if desired.

PREPARATION AND COOKING TIME: 45 minutes
YIELD: 4-6 servings

INDEX

90

JLSN Books
The Junior League of Stamford-Norwalk, Inc.
748 Post Road
Darien, Connecticut 06820

Please send_____additional copies of OFF THE HOOK
    at $14.95 each. $_____
Conn. residents add sales tax of $1.12 each. $_____
Plus postage and handling of $1.75 each. $_____
Please gift wrap at $1.00 each. $_____
Make checks payable to   TOTAL $_____
OFF THE HOOK—JLSN Books.

Mail to:
Name_____
Address_____
City_____State_____Zip Code_____

————————⬗————————

JLSN Books
The Junior League of Stamford-Norwalk, Inc.
748 Post Road
Darien, Connecticut 06820

Please send_____additional copies of OFF THE HOOK
    at $14.95 each. $_____
Conn. residents add sales tax of $1.12 each. $_____
Plus postage and handling of $1.75 each. $_____
Please gift wrap at $1.00 each. $_____
Make checks payable to   TOTAL $_____
OFF THE HOOK—JLSN Books.

Mail to:
Name_____
Address_____
City_____State_____Zip Code_____

Gift wrap and send to the following:
Name_____
Address_____
City_____State_____Zip Code_____
Gift card to read:_____
_____

Gift wrap and send to the following:
Name_____
Address_____
City_____State_____Zip Code_____
Gift card to read:_____
_____

—————————————— 🐟 ——————————————

Gift wrap and send to the following:
Name_____
Address_____
City_____State_____Zip Code_____
Gift card to read:_____
_____

Gift wrap and send to the following:
Name_____
Address_____
City_____State_____Zip Code_____
Gift card to read:_____
_____